T0160886

RUSTY BARBED WIRE

Books by David Lee

The Porcine Legacy (1978)
Driving and Drinking (1979)
The Porcine Canticles (1984)
Day's Work (1990)
Paragonah Canyon (1990)
My Town (1995)
Covenants (with William Kloefkorn) (1996)
The Fish (1997)
Wayburne Pig (1997)
A Legacy of Shadows (1999)
News From Down to the Café (1999)
Incident at Thompson Slough (2002)
So Quietly the Earth (2004)
Texas Wild Flowers (2011)
In a House Made of Time (with William Kloefkorn)(2010)
Stone   Wind   Water (2011)
Moments of Delicate Balance
(with William Kloefkorn) (2011)
Last Call (2014)
Bluebonnets, Firewheels and Brown Eyed Susans (2017)
Mine Tailings (2019)
The Allegory of Perfection (2020)

RUSTY BARBED WIRE

SELECTED POEMS

DAVID LEE

Samara Press
2022

ISBN 978-1-955140-00-3
Library of Congress Control Number: 2021946906
Printed in the United States of America
Samara Press
www.samarapress.net
Cover painting by Phyllis Shafer
Designed by Robert E. Blesse

For

Jan
Mi regalo las bodas de oro
No lo habria logrado sin ti

&
Jon and JoDee

Con amor

CONTENTS

THE PORCINE LEGACY

LOADING A BOAR

We were loading a boar, a goddam mean big sonofabitch and he
jumped out of the pickup four times and tore out my stockracks and
rooted me in the stomach and I fell down and he bit John on the
knee and he thought it was broken and so did I and the boar stood
over in the far corner of the pen and watched us and John and I just
sat there tired and Jan laughed and brought us a beer and I said,
"John it's not worth it, nothing's going right and I'm feeling half dead
and haven't written a poem in ages and I'm ready to quit it all," and
John said, "shit, young feller, you aint got started yet and the reason's
cause you trying to do it outside yourself and aint looking in and if
you wanna by god write pomes you gotta write pomes about what
you know and not about the rest and you can write about pigs and
that boar and Jan and you and me and the rest and there aint no way
you're gonna quit," and we drank beer and smoked, all three of us,
and finally loaded that mean bastard and drove home and unloaded
him and he bit me again and I went in the house and got out my paper
and pencils and started writing and found out John he was right.

BEHOLD

And came forth like Venus from an ocean of
heat waves, morning in his pockets and the buckets in his hands
he emerged from the gray shed, tobacco and wind
pursed together in song from his tight lips he gathered day
and went out to cast wheat before swine. And in
his mind he sang songs and thought thoughts, images of clay
and heat, wind and sweat, dreams of silver and
visions of green earth twisting the cups of his mind
he crossed his fence of rusty barbed wire, the south Utah steppes
bending the air into corners of sky he entered
the yard to feed his swine. And his pigs, they come.

Jubilate Agno, 1975

Christopher Smart, 1722-1771
Blackula Poland China, 1971-1975
(memorandus)

For I will consider my black sow Blackula.
For she is the servant of the god of the feed bucket and serveth him.
For she worships the god in him and the secret of his pail in her way.
For this is done by screams of incantation at the appointed hour and
    lusty bites of daily communion.
For she stands with forelegs upon the top rail of the wooden fence in supplication.
For she grunts her thanks while she eats.
For she stands for the red boar with closed eyes at the appointed hour.
For having done she lies in the mud to consider herself.
For this she performs in ten degrees.
For first she rolls in her wallow to cover her body.
For secondly she lies still to feel the wet.
For thirdly she stretches her length and casts her belly to the sun.
For fourthly she exhales God's air in huge sighs.
For fifthly she rises and examines her feed trough that replenishment
    might miraculously appear.
For sixthly she scratches her side against the fence.
For seventhly she scratches her jowl with delicate pastern swipe.
For eighthly she smells the breeze to ascertain the red boar's presence.
For ninthly she returns to her mud and plows large holes in the earth.
For tenthly she lies again in the wallow to cool her frame.
For having considered her world she will sleep and dream dreams of
    herself and her god and the red boar.
For like Eve for softness she and sweet attractive Grace was formed.
For the red boar lusteth mightily and foameth at the mouth for her.
For he might escape and enter her pen.
For if he does this in a nonappointed hour she will scream loudly
    and discourage his kisses.
For her belly is full and needeth no more.
For in one month she will bring forth life in abundance.
For in her last litter she farrowed eight piglets of the red boar.
For three were black and five were red.

For she raised them all and laid on none.
For one in eight is normally crushed by the sow.
For she is exceedingly good in all that she does.
For she is surely of the tribe of Elephant and forgetteth not.
For she weighs near six hundred pounds.
For she has ears of tremendous size.
For she is heavy.
For a large sow is a term of the Titan Elephant.
For she has the appetite of a bird and would eat the day long which
    in debt her master suppresses.
For he would not have her too fat or his checkbook hollow.
For he keeps her well-fed and she breaks no fence.
For she grunts in pleasure from the mud when he scratches her ears.
For she is a tool of God to temper his mind.
For when she eats her corn she turns and shits in her trough.
For her master is provoked but hereby learns patience.
For she is an instrument for him to learn bankruptcy upon.
For he lost but four dollars each on the last litter of pigs.
For this is admirable in the world of the bank.
For every man is incomplete without one serious debt or loss.
For she provides this with her good faith.
For every farm is a skeleton without a mortgage.
For the Lord admonished black sows when he said lay up no stores
    of treasure on earth.
For she prohibits this daily.
For she is a true child of God and creature of the universe.
For she is called Blackula which is a derivative of the Devil, but false.
For she does worship her God and Savior.
For she was given her name for breaking a fence and eating Jan's
    garden beets.
For when Jan came with a stick and wrath she lifted her head and smiled.
For her teeth and mouth were stained with red beet pulp.
For Jan dropped the stick and laughed.
For she looked like a six-hundred-pound vampire.
For she was called Blackula.
For we feed her red beets daily to watch her smile.
For she is humble when well-fed.
For she makes her point well when she is hungry.
For there is nothing swifter than a sow breaking fence when she desires.

For there is nothing more beautiful than a sow in full run when being chased through a garden.

For there is no sound more pure than her scream when she is hit with a stick.

For she is meek in all aspects when satisfied.

For when John Sims saw her lying in mud he proclaimed her majesty.

For he whistled and called her a pretty sonofabitch.

For he offered to trade his beat-up truck for her straight across.

For she has divine spirit and is manifest as a complete pig.

For she is tame and can be taught.

For she can run and walk and sleep and drink and eat.

For she can scream at the red boar.

For she allows her ears and belly to be scratched.

For she allows small children to ride her back.

For she sleeps in mounds of straw at night.

For she produces litters of healthy black and red pigs.

For she can root the earth.

For she can carry sticks in her mouth.

For she will grunt when she is addressed.

For she can jump not far but hard.

For dried earth cracks in the places where she walks.

For she is hated by the breeders of cattle and sheep.

For the former loses more money than I do on his stock.

For the latter fears her mind.

For she has no wool and will not blindly follow his steps.

For he carries no bucket of feed.

For she litters twice per year.

For he litters but once.

For her belly is firm and can take much abuse.

For from this proceeds her worth.

For I perceive God's mystery by stroking her teats.

For I felt tiny lumps of flesh within and knew they were alive.

For the life is the physical substance which God sends from Heaven to sustain the appetites of men.

For God has blessed her womb and the red boar's seed.

For they multiply in ecstasy at the appointed time.

For God has blessed her in many ways.

For God has given her the red beets to eat.

For God has given the water for her to drink.

For God has allowed the water to run to mud in a place for her to lay.

For she cannot fly to the mountain streams, though she walks well
upon the earth.
For she walks the earth heavy upon tiny feet.
For she treads all the rows of the summer garden.
For she can jump the fence.
For she can push it down.
For she can eat.

RACEHOGS

John calls and sez Dave
when I say hello and I say hello John
and he sez come down Dave
you gotta see what I got
I say fine I'll be right there and he sez
bring Jan I'll show her too
and I said I will
so Jan and I got in the car to see
what John bought.
John bought four hogs
starved half to death, bones out
everywhere, snouts sharp enough
to root pine trees and the longest damn legs
I've seen. What do you think? he sez
and I don't say anything so he sez
I sez what do you think? and I say
them's pretty good-looking racehogs John
and he sez what? and I tell him
I heard about a place in Japan or California
(because he's never been there) where they
have a track and race hogs
on Tuesday nights and he sez do they
pay much? and I say yes or so I heard
maybe a hundred to win and he sez
goddam and I say those hogs
ought to be good with them long legs
and skinny bodies and he sez goddam.
Jan's walked off so I go find her
but she's mad and says I ought not to do that
and I say oh I was just bullshitting
but when we come back John's standing
by the fence throwing little pieces of feed
all around the pen making the hogs
hurry from one place to the next
and when I get up close he's smiling
and I can hear him whisper
while he throws the feed
run you skinny fuckers, run.

For Jan, with Love

1

John he comes to my house
pulls his beat up truck in my drive
and honks
Dave John sez Dave my red sow
she got pigs stuck and my big hands they won't go
and I gotta get them pigs out
or that fucker shes gonna die
and I sez John goddam
we'll be right down and John sez Jan
he yells JAN where's Jan she's got little hands
she can get in there and pull them pigs
and I sez Jan and he sez Jan and Jan comes
what? Jan sez and John sez tell Jan Dave
and I sez Jan John's red sow's got pigs
stuck and his hand's too big and won't go
and he's gotta get them pigs out
or that fucker's gonna die (John he turns
his head and lights a cigarette)
(he don't say fuck to no woman)
and Jan she sez well let's go
and we get in John's beat up damn truck
and go to pull John's pigs

2

John's red sow she doesn't weigh
a hundred and sixty pounds
but he bred her to his biggest boar
and had to put hay bales by her sides
so the boar wouldn't break
her back because Carl bet five dollars
he couldn't and John he bet
five she could and John he won
but Carl enjoyed watching anyway

3

John's red sow was laying
on her side hurting bad
and we could see she had a pig
right there but it wouldn't come she
was too small and John sez see
and I sez I see that pig's gotta come out
or that fucker's gonna die
and Jan puts vaseline on her hands
and sez hold her legs and I hold her legs
and Jan goes in after the pig
and John gets out of the pen and goes
somewheres else

Jan she pulls like hell pretty soon
the pig come big damn big little pig
dead and I give Jan more vaseline and she goes
back to see about any more
and John's red sow pushes hard on Jan's arm
up to her elbow inside and Jan sez
there's more help me and I help
another pig damn big damn dead comes
and John's red sow she seems better
and we hope that's all

4

John's red sow won't go
out of labor so we stay all night
and John brings coffee and smokes
and flashlight batteries and finally Jan
can feel another pig but John's red sow's
swole up tight and she can't grab hold
but only touch so I push her side
and she grunts and screams and shits all over Jan's arm
and Jan sez I got it help me and I help
and we pull for a goddam hour and pull
the pig's head off
and I sez oh my god we gotta get that pig out now

or that fucker's gonna die for sure
and John sez what happened? and Jan
gives him a baby pig's head in his hand
and John goes somewheres else again
while Jan goes back fast inside
grabbing hard and John's red sow
hurts bad and Jan sez I got something help me
and I help and we start taking that pig out
piece by piece

5

Goddamn you bitch don't you die
Jan yells when John's red sow don't help no more
and we work and the sun comes up
and we finally get the last piece of pig out
and give John's red sow a big shot of penicillin
her ass swole up like a football
but she don't labor and John sez
is that all? and Jan wipes her bloody arms
on a rag and sez yes and John climbs in
the pen and sez hows my red sow?
and we look and go home and go to bed
because John's red sow that fucker she died

A Day of Mourning, 24 November '75

I had to sell my black sow Blackula today.
She has become fallow, rejects the boar,
has no pigs and eats too much to keep.
Alas, goddammit. I loved that pig.

THE PORCINE CANTICLES

Tuesday Morning Loading Pigs

The worse goddam job of all
sez John pushing a thick slat
in front of the posts
behind the sow in the loading chute
so when she balked and backed up
she couldn't turn and get away
I never seen a sow or a hog load easy
some boars will
mebbe it's because they got balls
or something I don't know
but I seen them do it
that Brown feller the FFA
he's got this boar he just opens the trailer door
he comes and gets in
course he mebbe knows what
he's being loaded up for

it was this Ivie boy back home
the best I ever seen for loading
he wasn't scared of nothing
he'd get right in and shove them up
he put sixteen top hogs
in the back of a Studebaker pickup
by hisself I seen it

when he was a boy he opened up
the tank on the tractor
smelling gas
made his brains go soft they sed
he failed fifth grade
but it wasn't his fault
he could load up hogs

I always had to at home
cause I was the youngest
I sed then it was two things

I wouldn't do when I grown up
warsh no dishes or load up hogs
by god they can set in the sink
a month before I'll warsh them
a man's got to have a principle
he can live by is what I say
now you grab her ears and pull
I'll push from back here
we'll get that sonofabitch in the truck

Tuesday Morning,
Driving to the Auction in Salina

Sometimes sez John
it's so pretty here I caint stand it
I'm on that hay swoker
it's green alfalfa all in front
and then them red Utah hills behind
climb up to the mountains
just like they're pasted on blue

but then it's times I'm alone I listen past it all
I hear Misippi
like a big muscle holding its blood
and the slosh on them rotten piles
down behind the house at night
I can almost see
that moon trying to push up the sky
reflected off the water
and the clouds fall apart
like pieces of paint
coming off old walls in the bedroom
it's almost the taste of fog
floating down the river
behind the cold nightwind
you know what I mean?

and John drove in silence
thinking me asleep
as I stared out toward the shrouded river
a thousand miles distant
listened to the sliding brown water
move over the etched memory
of a red-and-white bobber
dancing on the ripples of my mind

The Muffler and the Law

1

You got a sow in heat? John sez
this morning when he called
I sed oh yas John I got four right now
John sez it wouldn't one
be that big black one would it?
I sed yas she's in I'm going to turn her
in with the boar this afternoon
John sez I'll be right down
to get her I want to borrow that sow
he hung up

John brought his beatup truck
to my house with his big spotted boar
loaded in the back and a partition
so another hog could be put in
but the boar couldn't get to it
he drove right out to my loading chute
by the time I got there
John was trying to load up my big black sow
I sed John what are you doing?
John looked at me like I was crazy
he sez you gonna hep me or stand there?
I didn't say anything else
I helped John load up my big black sow
and John drove off with her
in his truck he never did say where

2

Late afternoon John drove up
to my house he honks
he yells Dave come hep me unload
this big black sow of yours
she's done bred

I don't need her no more
he drives out back
to the loading chute
and unloads the sow
before I can get there

3

John I sed what the hell's going on
I mean you come get my big black sow
drive off without telling me anything
and you bring her back bred
to your spotted boar
what if I didn't want her bred to him?
John sez no charge
so it was all right then
I was going to tell him he could take
the other three sows that were in
for a ride all day tomorrow if he wanted
but John shut the gate on his stock racks
and sat down on his tailgate

it was this deputy sheriff
John sez so I said which? John sez
that one in Richfield
last week going to the auction in Salina
I run over this rockslide
on the cutoff by Cove Fort
I busted my muffler pipe aloost
and all the brackets I had to stop
on the summit and fix it all up
with bailing wire
it took an hour almost and I was late
for the auction so I had to go
the muffler was loost
and it made a noise
but I didn't have no more time
I had to hurry
I got to Richfield
here comes this law

his red lights on and his siren honking
right in the middle of town
I got out and sez I'm late to the auction
he slams his car door and put his hand
on it he puts his other hand right down
on his gun sez I don't know whar
YOU from mister but in MY town
we got a law here
I'm standing there with a truckload of hogs
people driving by slow looking at me
right in the middle of Richfield
I sez I'm late to the auction again
what I done wrong this time?
he sez in my town we got a law
against loud mufflers so you gone have
to pay you a fine for it mister
I sez look I done hit this rock slide
coming and busted
I tried to wire it up but couldn't
you look under here you can see
I'm late to the auction
his red lights was still going

I bent down to show him the wire underneath
he jumped in his car and taken out
his microphone he called this other law
so I stood up he sez you stand right there
I sez whar? he sez right there
he jumps out his car and puts his hand
on his gun again sez you trying
to resist arrest on me
I sez no I'm trying to show you
the bailing wire under here
holding up the pipes and the muffler
where I hit the rock on the mountain
but I caint hold the muffler on right
and the auction starts in fifteen minutes
he sez you just stand right there still
I got a reaforcement coming
we gone arrest you

4

I sed what happened John? John
sez the other law he come
and they both wrote me out a ticket
for loud mufflers and resisting arrest
and the other one that come
sez he believed I was speeding too
but they never wrote a ticket for it
and that's too bad cause I was
I was late for the auction

I sez can I go now but the law
he sez you got to pay your fine
I sez the auction started five minutes ago
and I got to get there
the other law he sez why you
going to the auction you selling hogs?
I never sez a word to that dumb sonofabitch
he's standing right there by my truck
loaded up with twelve top hogs
wallering each other in the middle of town
all the cars driving by watching
the first law sez you got to foller us
to the J.P. I sez isn't it no other way?
he sez you trying to bribe a officer of the law?
I sez hell no I'm trying to get to the auction
the other law sez whar?
and the first sez Salina they sell hogs at one
I sez that was ten minutes ago
the other law sez you selling these hogs?
but I wasn't talking to him
the law sez you want a regular judge
you can come back next Friday
but the fine goes up for that
I sez can I go now? and the law sez yas
but the other one sez not till you
get that muffler fix

I had to get my truck towed
to a filling station four blocks away
and the muffler pipe welted
he charged me forty-seven dollars
and sixty-five cents to do it
I could have done it for a dollar
at home if I had my tools
by then the auction was over
I had to drive all them pigs home
after I'd loaded them up that morning
to take to the auction at Salina

5

I sed that's too bad John
John sez I couldn't sleep about it
for a man to talk to me that way
all he had to done was look
under the truck so he could see
it wasn't my fault
I tried to fix it best I could

he sez the fine would go up
so I sez to myself John it's done costed
fifty dollars almost so you
might as well get your say out of it
but I didn't have no sow in heat
so that's how come I called you

I sed John I don't understand
John sez I drove to Richfield
with that panel between the hogs
my spotted boar he about chewed it
in two trying to get to your big black sow
but he couldn't so I went right to the spot
where that law pulled me over
in the middle of town
I stopped my truck and got out
climbed up on my stockracks
I took out the panel
let the boar go to her

I sed you did what? John sez
by god she wasn't quite ready yet
she squolt and here come the cars to see
I bet they could hear her half a mile
and here come the law
with his red light on
he sez what the hell are you doing?
I sez I'm here to pay my fine
he sez you get that truck out of here
with them pigs people's watching
I sez whar? he waved his arms he sez
everwhar see them they all coming
I sez I got to pay my fine I come to go
to court he sez whar? I sez right here
lord it was horrible my spotted boar
he slobbered all over your black sow
it was hog slobber on both her ears
that law he's as red in the face

as a fox's ass he couldn't do nothing
he finally sez you get in your truck
you foller me I sez that's fine
but you go slow I got a load of hogs in mine
I caint be jostling them any
we drove to the courthouse

6

Judge he says what's going on?
law he sez you honor he's disturbing peace
Judge he sez how? law he sez
he's got these pigs in his truck
and they copperlating in the middle of town
Judge he sez whar? law he sez
right out there so Judge gets up
he looks out his winder there's my truck
but now my spotted boar he's done
he lain down he wasn't getting up
pooped Judge sez all I see is a hog
law he sez but they was scruting!
Judge he sez don't you ever talk that way

in a court of law you hear me?
all I see is a hog and it isn't no law
that sez this man caint haul no hog
through town in his truck
we haven't made that one yet
so I sez your honor I want you to listen
to my side of this so I told him
the whole story about the muffler
and the law how I missed the auction
he looks at that law he sez
is it the way it happened like he sez?
law he commenced to squirming
but he has to say yassir your honor finally
I told him how it costed me fifty dollars almost
to get it fix and I had to be towed
four blocks with twelve top hogs in the truck
Judge he sez cased dismissed and he sez
to me he's sorry about it all
specially the fifty dollars so I sez it's the way it is
caint be nothing done now
I didn't have no more hard feelings
so we shaken hands and I left

law he's mad as hell outside waiting
he sez mister you ever come to my town again
I'll make you sweat I'll
arrest your ass and throw you in jail
I sez mister deputy sheriff law
you listen here you listen good
you ever bother me again for anything
next time I'll pull a trailer and bring
eight sows and three boars all together I'll park
in front of the schoolhouse and take out the panel
I'll go in and tell them you sez for me
to meet you there and where are you
you posta have the money for me for them hogs
if you don't believe it you just try
and I sez then so you just get out of my way
I walked on past him and went and left
he never sez one more word to me

7

so here's your big black sow
John sed and he stood up
she's done bred to my spotted boar
but you don't owe me nothing
I aint never won one with the law before
so I reckon this one's on me
John closed his tailgate and leaned in
and patted his spotted boar
on the head and then John got in
his beat up truck and drove home for supper

MEAN

Hell Hath No Fury Like a Sow with Pigs

1

Pretty soon now I sed and
John nods his head watching
so I sed I see she's broken the sack
there's water and his head goes up and down
again but he doesn't say anything
so we both stand and watch
John's big white sow back in her shed
while she breathes easy
seven hundred pounds sprawled across yellow straw
finally John sez any time now
and I nod my head this time
he sez yep just any time
but the only thing we can do is watch
so we stand and wait
and watch John's white sow labor
and John lights a cigarette
to help the time go by while we watch

2

Last time sez John she went crazier'n hell
I had her in that pen with a wood floor
I put in a lamp for the cold and
she's half done and got up that mean sonofabitch
she done went over and bit that lectric wire
and it shocked her or something
she went like a crazy womern to banging
her head on the walls and floor
and hollered like a elephant shot in the butt
with buckshot she tore hell out of that pen
and had two more pigs while she's standing up
and never knew it she acted like she's blind
and couldn't see nothing I had to get
them pigs out with a rake or she'd of stomped

on them all she jerked that rake
right out of my hand twicet I had
to get it back with a stick so's I could get
them pigs out or they'd be dead
I got all but one that she killed
and she finally went over and lain down
to have her pigs again but ever time
one of them I had out squolt she'd jump up
and go crazy again I had to put them pigs
in the front of my pickup all night
to make her be still and that light
never did work after that she ruint it
so I sez how come you keep her John?
she's too big and mean and John
looks at me like I was nuts or something
he sed cause she had twelve pigs and raised
all but one more besides the one she stomped
that's why, wouldn't you? but I didn't
say anything, John's white sow was too mean
for me, I would have sold her to John
if she was mine but she wasn't
she was already John's so I didn't have to

3

John I sez after awhile because she wouldn't pig
I'll bet that sow's got a pig stuck breech
and it won't come but John looks over
at his pickup and doesn't say anything
so I say if she does and it doesn't come
it could kill her and all them pigs too
don't you think? but he keeps looking at
his pickup so I say I don't know of course
but that might be it she's been in labor
a long time and she broke her water
before I got here I saw the last of the wet
when I came but I don't know she's not my sow
it might not be that but John sez real low
she throwed Carl out of the pen that time
he got in and tried to climb out after him

she'd of killed him if she'd got to him
so I decided I wouldn't say anything else
she was John's sow and he'd know what to do

4

Why don't you get in there and look
sez John you know more about that than I do
and I sez no I don't John and I have
to be getting home pretty soon Jan will be
getting worried and I hate to keep
her up John sez Dave I'll give you twenty-five
dollars if you'll go get that pig out and
I sez John I'm not getting in that pen with
that sow for a hundred dollars John sez
okay fifteen dollars cash I sez no John
I'm not going to get in there for a thousand
dollars John sez I'll give you a pig
I sez I wouldn't do it for the sow and all
the pigs loaded up to take to the auction
John sez okay a live pig and you can pick it
but I sed no and I meant it
not for all his pigs and I acted like I
was getting ready to leave
I wasn't I wanted to see how it came out
but I wasn't getting in that pen
so John goddammed me and sed I was a sissy
and I didn't say anything because John was right

5

John sez if I get in there will you come
and hold the lantern in the door so I can see?
and I sed yas because the sow was in
bad shape by then we could see that and
she had to have help but I sed John
if she comes after me I'm getting out
and I'm not going to worry about the lantern
getting out with me so it may get busted
John sez if she gets up you just make sure

you don't get in my way or she'll get you
and the lantern both and I sed okay
because I knew there's no way John
can get out of that pen before me
I wasn't worried about that
so I sed where's the lantern? John sez
over here so we go to his pickup
for the lantern and John gives me the lantern
and some clean rags to hold then
he gets in his jockey box and pulls out
a pistol I sez what's that? and John sez
it's a gun and I sez ohIsee and he sez
I aint getting in there with her without no
gun my mama didn't raise no idiots
and if I need this I want to have it
with me that's why and he put it in
his coat pocket and I didn't say anything
because she wasn't my sow she was John's

6

John climbed in the pen and I followed
he went in the shed with the sow but I
stayed in the door while he moved around
behind her slow to see what she'd do
she had her eyes closed and breathed
hard because she hurt so bad
and I shined the light in so John could see
John knelt down behind her and touched her
but she didn't move so he rolled up his sleeve
and started in to see what was wrong
breech? I whispered and he nodded so
I was right and John went in to try and get it out
John whispers hold still I caint see
and I sez who? and he sez you and
I saw the lantern was shaking I was scared
so I held it with both hands and it was still
John twisted his hand inside the sow
and he sed I got it I'm gone take it out now
he started pulling his arm back and the

pig came out and it was breech
got it? I sed and John sez yas gimme a rag
and I leaned in to hand him a towel and
the pig wiggled in his hand John tried to grab
its mouth but the pig squealed in his hand

7

Goddam you John screamed
the white sow jumped up and bellowed
so loud the tin roof on the shed shook
and jerked around toward John
I stood there like Lot's wife shining the light in
John screams goddam you again
and jumps back against the back wall
of the shed and hits it so hard it should have
come down holding the pig tight against his chest
the sow roars at him the muscles
in her body standing out all the hair on
her back straight up and I think drop that pig
John but I can't say anything I'm frozen
holding the lantern in the door
the sow roaring and John screaming
then he tears at his pocket and pulls out
the pistol goddam you he yells you get away from me
you sonofabitch and the sow barks loud like a maddog
the size of a jersey cow
John points the pistol at her head and it shakes
like an aspen limb in springtime
goddam you and she screams again
snick snick snick snick snick snick snick
I see the empty cylinder turn as John pulls
the trigger and I taste powder in my mouth
drop it! I hear somebody say
John keeps pulling the trigger yelling goddam you
the sow roars and her shoulders bunch up in a knot
she's so mad she's slobbering
DROP IT I yell again and John looks at me
his eyes wide as hubcaps
DROP THAT PIG I scream and I see John's

hand loosen and the pig falls to the ground
but he keeps pulling the trigger snicksnicksnick
the pig hits on its back and lies there
and the sow lowers her head and looks at it
but keeps on grunting loud and mean and fast
John stops pulling the trigger but keeps the pistol
pointed at her head and the pig gets up
and starts moving the sow quits grunting and
sniffs it then looks at John and barks again
John pulls the trigger again but he can't
say anything anymore and the sow turns and lies down
and grunts and another pig pops out
the first pig finds her and tries to find a teat
and the second pig squirms and shakes its head and
tries to clear its nose and John stands with
the pistol pointed at the sow and I stand
holding the lantern and the sow grunts to her pigs
just like we're not there and nothing happened
and I say John? and John points the pistol at me
I say get out John and he sez whar?
and I say get out of that shed John before
she gets up and John sez who? and I say
get out of there John and John looks at the sow
and points the pistol at her and he starts
sliding around the wall and we get out
of John's mean white sow's pen

8

John's shaking so hard he can't light
a cigarette so I do it but he drops it on
the floorboard and I pick it up and put it
in his mouth and he smokes
I say you got a beer? and he sez in the back
I think so I take the lantern and look
and he has some hid in his junk in the bed
I get it and for a long time we drink beer
and don't say anything and I see that my hands
are shaking so the beer foams out the top of my can
so I drink three fast so it won't
and I don't know if he ever finished his

finally I sed John I wouldn't have a pig like that
I'd get rid of her if she's mine she's just too mean
she's gonna kill somebody someday
John's staring straight ahead through the window
the muscles in his face still tight, drawn
he sez goddammit that's too bad
and I sed well you can't help it some go mean
he sez she was a good sow I sez she's okay now
John sez but it was her or me and I sez it's okay John
he sips his beer then sets it on the dashboard
and leans back and I see tears in his eyes and
he's still staring straight ahead through the windshield
she was a good sow he sez even if she was mean
goddammit I hated having to shoot her like that
and I looked out the window and didn't
say anything. She was John's sow, not mine.

THE FARM

We sold it. To a man
who would be a patriarch.
I told John we were closed in,
subdivisions and trailers all around,
complaints of the smell (though
there was none), Ira came out
and told me to keep them fenced
(though none broke out), the neighbors
frightened because someone's cousin's
friend heard of a hog
that ate a child who fell in the pen (though
their children rode my sows
at feeding time), because I was tired,
because Jan carried our child and could
no longer help, because she wanted a home.

And the patriarch lost his first crop
to weeds, threw a rod in the tractor,
dug a basement and moved the trailer on
for extra bedrooms, cut the water lines
for a ditch, subdivided the farm
and sold the pigs for sausage. I told John
they were his, they were no longer mine,
I couldn't be responsible.

The wire connecting our voices was silent
for a moment. "You stupid sonofabitch," was all
he finally said. "You poor stupid bastard."

Aftermath

There were pigs
in the night, a wild herd
overran the farm, trampled
my fences and flowers, rooted the garden.
Lost in the depths of overturned garbage cans,
their grunts echo in the darkness
as they search the land
while the night reaches out before them
like a starving child.

Jan nudged me awake
to the walls of this new place we call
home. "It's all right," she said
and slept. And I lay awake
the rest of the night, listening
as the wind carried the scraps of sound
bounced them against the house,
muffled grunts of the abandoned herd
searching us out in the night.

EPILOGUE

> What might have been and what has been
> Point to one end, which is always present.
> —T.S. Eliot,"Burnt Norton"
>
> In my beginning is my end ...
> In my end is my beginning.
> —T.S. Eliot, "East Coker"

Months begat seasons begat a year
another
begat a child, another
begat all the successes: advancement,
rank, salary equal to almost one-
half the yearly inflation,
begat respectability, political acumen

voted for all the losers,
Ananias Frogeyes elected, reelected, scholarly insight
studied the use of feminine endings in Milton
by the book, rocked no boats
therefore happy was Dave, indeed, passive

Jan made it official,
asked: are you happy?
replied: of course. Why not?
asked: are you sure?
replied: I'm very busy. Is there something you need?

And on Saturday Jan left
for groceries, I baby-sat
studied scientific humanism, read essays
she returned, honked
honked, honked
until outside came Dave, passive
said get this sonofbitch unloaded
replied: I beg your pardon
said either get it unloaded

or go back and set on your butt
I'll do it

Saw in the pickup bed
fence wire, twenty cedar posts, sheet iron,
one dozen 2x6 boards, a gunnysack
behold, a gunnysack, tow sack
tied with a strand of wire
baliwore I've seen that before
a voice whispered, where have you been,
Jan? Jan where have you …
tow sack while I watched
            moved

And I known
I known whatall's in that towsack's
trouble, break any fence
any man can build or fix
lay in the mud, dig holes
belly up to the sun, eat
anything can be eat, gnaw
whatall'll hold still to be gnawed
piss me off worse'n anything alive
bring out all the worse
all the best
            in me

behind the spare tire another sack
behold squirmed
tow sack moved, rolled, tow sack
squealed, squirmed, rooted, tow sack
tied with baliwore grunted
but it caint holt it long
don't worry about being polite
you got to hurry
it'll get out goddam
            another one

DAY'S WORK

After an All-Night Farrow

The thin moon
burns silver
in henlight

Then gold lace
falls like dew
on the sheet-iron roof

Now sun sprays
the pasture
and the duroc boar's shoulders
with fire

Rooster: flap your wings!
Scratch up
a breakfast song
for these eight
newborn children

SONNET ON THE SUN RISING

Cold. Last night a skiff
of snow. So I
got up five o'clock, made
a fire. Watched the sky
                unbuild.

I mean, I'm
drinking coffee
      by myself. Shivering.

And I'm cold.
    So it's time, you
    wonderful sun
of a bitch. Get on up.
        I'm ready.
            Now.

Arthritis

for Ken and Bobbie

Can you come help me a minute?
Take and grab this thing right here,
now put them pliers on it there
and hold, I'll get a clamp on
wait a minute, just hang on
right there, yep, there. Okay
youg'n leggo it's done and I thank you

I caint grab holt of nothing tight
today my arthritises is bad
and I haven't got no grip
I swallered four aspurns for breakfast
but they aint working yet
I wisht I had me a copper bracelet
they say helps out when you got it on
or one of them Mexican chinchilla dogs
you can set with it in your lap
and watch TV and it keeps
the arthritis away

Ruby Patrick back home had one
she's Kay Stokes's daughter
married this Jack Patrick rancher
he hit oil everywhere he stuck a stick
in the ground just like Kay Stokes done
so she's rich on both sides
but she had arthritis anyway
in her fingers and toes I heard
went all over to them specialists doctors
spent a damn backseat full of money
to find out they couldn't do nothing
and then asked old man Cummings
who could take warts off of you
what to do cause he'd know

he sez get you one of them Meskin
dogs without no hair on it that can fit
in a teacup they advertise in Grit
and the funny books and set with it
in your lap a hour a day
and it'll be a whole lot better
but it won't never go away
you might as well get a marriage license
to it so she did

I heard she paid a hundred dollars
for that dog and got papers
to prove it was a real one so
when Kay Stokes heard about it
he thrown a fit till his face swole up
like a tomater sez what the hell
goddam good is that thing?
he had half the money in the world
but a hundred dollars for a dog like that
was one too many for him that day
can it hunt? he sez can it swim?
can it bring back a duck or a quail?
that sonofabitch caint even set up
in the front seat of a pickup
and see out the winder
what possessed you to pay good money
for a little shiteater fycet?
she sed you get out of here right now
it's none of your bidness what I do
and it's not one penny out of your pockets
so you don't have nothing to say about it.
Any penny spent in this town he sed
is a penny that could of been mine
but he went and left anyway
he never did like that dog
but that was okay
that dog never had no love
for him either

she'd set on the furniture
in her living room with that thing
on her leg and if anybody come in
it'd commence to growl and shake
all over, its lip would come up
eyes'd bug out like grapes
on a mustang vine
that dog known in its heart
it could whup anything alive
that come in or around its house
or the car if it was in it
you could set there and talk to her
for a hour or shell peas all morning
that dog'd never take its eyes off you
or quit snarling, it didn't like nobody
except her and that included her husband
but she sed it did help her arthritis
and she liked it so there you go

then these sorry poor people
come to town in a whole carload
it must of been a dozen of them it seemed
we figgered they traveled from one town
to anothen looking for handouts
after they left
nobody got a for sure count
on all them kids
but it didn't seem no way
he could of got the back winders
in his car closed
he'd of had to cut off seven arms
and a leg and three heads

they showed up at the churchhouse
Sunday morning and sed
they want to join up, man sez
he wants to address the congergation
sed my kids aint ate a good meal
in a week now what y'all

gone do about it, brothers and sisters?
wasn't nothing they could do
except have a prayer and take up
a collection but they didn't get much
so somebody sez I think it was
Billie Hill we could bring them back
some food this evening
at the prayer meeting so they did

Mizrez Patrick she brung twelve quart jars
of homecanned peaches she was proud of
she won the blue ribbon almost ever year
at the fair and sez I hope you enjoy them
but could I please have the jars back
when you done? she's polite that time
he sez yas ma'am whar do I brang them?
she sez address on the jarlabel
so they loaded it all up in his car
and he taken and drove off
didn't even stay for prayer meeting
next morning here he comes
up the street dragging a kid's wagon
nobody known where he got
probley stoled it with all them jars
in it empty none of them even warshed
and knocks on the door
she sed did you eat all that fruit arredy?
when she seen the wagon
on the sidewalk he sez
good godamiteychrist lady
when we eat fruit we eat fruit, by god
neighbors seen her
sed her face and jaw went so tight
she could of bit a hole in a crowbar
never sed nothing
went out the door and picked up three jars
in each hand and went in with them
then come back for the rest
he never offered to help her carry them

but when she come back he sez
anybody in there happen to have a cigarette?
she sed nobody in that house smokes
that I've ever heard of
he sez well that's your bidness
I expect not mine she sed it certainly is
shut the wooden door when she went in

he set down right by the yard gate
started picking his nose and whistling
like he worked there for them
for a living at their house
waiting, he's a professional
she seen it right then
through the windercurtains
he's gone wait her out till she come
and sed what do you want?
that's how come he had the wagon
to carry more back to where he come from
well he had the wrong lady
just cause she was expensive
lived in a big house
and had a fycet she was still
Kay Stokes's daughter and that dog
had papers to prove who he was
so she let the sun shine on him
all day till the afternoon
she opened the door a crack
he started to get up probley thought
she's gone offer him some lemonade
here come that dog out the door

he sez hey lady your shiteater
he never got to finish
that dog was on him
went around his ankle three times
torn his sock right off his leg
put a swok up the back his shirt
like a lawnmower run over him

lit in his hair
grapt a mouthful out and about dug
a hole in his head with his back feet
in about a second and a half
GODAMITEY SONOFABITCH he yelled
jumped up and tried to run
but the dog got in his eyes
and scratched his face
he put his foot in the wagon
and it took off the other way
he fell down on the fence
ripped his britches hollering like a elephant
with its tail in a knot
got up and run down the street
that dog chased him a block
bit him on the finger when he swatted
at it running never broke a stride
he's gone
they left the wagon right there
on the sidewalk for a week
where he turnt it over
but he never come back for it
nobody saw them again
so they give it to the school finally
she said Carlos!
that's what she called that dog
you come right back here in this house
right now, I didn't say
you could go outside
that dog spun round in the street
and went home like a whirlwind
was after him
went through that front door
right between her legs
and she shut it, it was all over
nobody ever heard what she sed
to that dog or about it
she never mentioned it again
but that dog held her arthritis down

for a many a many year
she'd set with it and pet it
in her lap and even Kay Stokes
sed it cut down on the doctor bills
and the aspurns from Bob Collier drug
but he never did say it was worth it
but then he wouldn't
he wouldn't give a inch for nothing

so I wouldn't mind having one
I'd go watch TV with it
and let you fix this damn bailer
I caint figger out why that feeder
don't work and I caint get this wing nut
unscrewed come help me
don't just stand there looking
I told you my fingers don't work today

EDNA MAE

Rufus was the town undertaker
and Edna Mae his wife
lived with him in the back
of the funeral home
where they had another door
it opened to Huffman furniture
he run that too
when it wasn't nobody dead to bury.

You could tell when somebody died
in town, here'd come Edna Mae
down the street wearing her gold
high-heeled shoes
she always wore to funerals
and her mink stole rain or sun
cold or hot she worn it
we all called it her evening gown
whole town would know
somebody's dead before we known
who it was when we seen
Edna Mae's gold high heels.
She helped Rufus out
with the funerals and dead bodies
putting on their clothes
pinning on the corsages and
getting them right
her and Rufus was artists they sed
and I spoze so
didn't matter how mashed up
they was them two could get them natural
so they just looked dead
and the coffin lid could be opened
at the churchhouse to see
even Edgar Turner and his head
was half shot off.

You'd go to the cemetery
after the funeral and at the end
of the line was Edna Mae
and the preacher and Rufus
to shake hands and help feel sorry to
all the family and watchers
she's as official as the sheriff.

So she died of the cancer finally
everybody wondered how
Rufus'd do it to her and then
without her and how he'd dress her
but when we got to the funeral
there she was in her box
wearing her mink stole
and the preacher sez she'd done
wrote out all the plans
for her funeral
and the sermon and the prayers
and the singers and the songs
and before we could even wonder
about it they had the first song
and if I live to be a hundred
I'll never forget it
them singing Oh Them Golden Slippers
at her funeral
and everybody who was there'll swear
to this day when they went by
her box at the end
she's smiling.

Pain

for William Kloefkorn

Now how'd you do that? sed John
and I told him
about the pickup being stuck
wouldn't start
how I got mad and put my back
against the front and started it rocking
then gave all I had
heard the discs rupture
even before I felt the blue pain
pick me up and throw me
on the ground
eyeball to antenna with a red ant
that crawled up my nose
and I didn't even care

I've never hurt that way I said
it was the worst pain a man could feel

Oh shit sed John it is not
you lain back down right now
how'd you like it if I taken
and pult on these tractor ropes
they got you hooked up to
wouldn't that hurt just as bad
or worst?
and what if that one fat nurse
name Martha Rae come in
pull down your covers
with her crapper pan again
sez lift up you gotta try some more
staring at you and you aint got
no underwears on?
you tell me that don't hurt some
and everbody comes in

sez well that aint so bad
mine was worst
or my brother torn his back up
like yours and he still caint walk
or he caint stand up straight
or his pecker still don't have no feeling
in it and that was twenty years ago
or the doctor come in
sez we gone have to operate on you
and everybody you known
sed don't let him cut you
you'll be cripple for life
their uncle he's in a wheelchair
ever since caint do nothing
slobbers down the front of his shirt
nothing below his neck works
all the doctor's fault
you won't never be the same no more
you gone tell me that aint the worst
to hear truestories like that
and you just laying on your butt
in the bed taking up space
from people that's really sick

no that aint the worse
it aint even the worse I heard of
I'll tell you about some pain
everybody knows about that feller
set down on a crapper
at Possom Kingdom Lake
got blackwidow spider bit
on his privates and the whole end of it
come off with the poison
but I known a man
had cancer in the mouth
hurt so bad he chewed
half his tongue off before he died
got blood poison and gangrene
anothern had to chop his leg off

with a hatchet to get out
of a beartrap or he'd froze to death
died anyway in a car wreck
going to his mother's funeral
a year later so it wasn't worth it
and old Dan Walker
when his tractor wouldn't start
hit it with a sledgehammer
missed and broke his shinbone
crawled a mile to his house
to call somebody for help
and they'd unhooked his phone
cause he's behind on the bill
that's pain

but they's some
that hurts a different way
sometimes even worse
it was this boy in the fifth grade
name George Mendietta
he would of stoled his daddy's pickup
given it to you
for this one little girl name Danella Hagins
to say hello to him
but he's a Mexican and that's too bad
for him back then
so he helt it in all year
here comes Valentine day
what'd he do? goes down
to Bob Collier drugstore
taken and bought her a box
of red Valentine candy and a card
given it to her at the class party
we all remembered
cause she cried and had to go to the nurse's office
she's so embarrassed to have a Mexican
do such a thing to her
he never come back to school the rest of the year
I think that hurt purdy good

that aint the worse
I known of
I hurt just as bad
over Thelma Lou Shackleford
when I's seventeen
we all went out to eat fish
we'd been messing around all day
it was that night I known
I loved that girl more'n life
we all order oysters and horse relish
cept Thelma Lou
she orders catfish and the man
sez you want that broil or fried ma'am?
she sez fried
I can still hear the way that sound
slid off the front of her tongue
I's so ashamed eating raw oysters
I couldn't hardly hold one
in my mouth and Tommy Wayne Clayborn
ate his and half of mine
slopped saucet all over the table
like a hog licking his fingers
I watched her eat every bite
of her fish begging myself John
ask her to go for a ride
but I's too ascairt
afraid she might say no or laugh
when she's through
Tommy Wayne sez come on Thelma Lou
let's go up Sawmill Road
she never sed a word
got up and walked off with him
it wasn't nothing I could do
but watch her go

and that's not the worse
Thelma Lou was my sister's bestfriend
I known for a fact
cause Thelma Lou told her

as a secret to be kept so
she told me
how when she's twelve and come in
first time how she never known
what it was
nobody done told her
she thought she's busted something
bleeding to death
she went in the kitchen told her mother
her mother never turnt around
sed you get out of this room
you shut the door behind you
caint you see I'm cooking supper
I think that's worse

but even worst than that
was Tommy Wayne Clayborn
knocked her up and I think he done it
that night I couldn't say nothing
on the Sawmill Road
they didn't know what to do
everbody in town known about it
before they got around to telling their folks
finally Tommy Wayne told
his daddy name Shirley Clayborn
he's the sheriff back then and a good one
about the toughest man in town
partly because of his name
you'd say morning Shirley
he'd look right in your eye
if it was sparkling any
it wouldn't be purdy quick
so Tommy Wayne told him
he said what you gone do, boy?
Tommy Wayne sez gone marry her, daddy
Shirley sed is that what you want?
Tommy Wayne sez yas she's a hell of a girl
and she was goddammit
Shirley Clayborn called her family over

they all talked it out and sez okay
if that's how it is
and nobody got his ast kicked
like he should of
when they left Tommy Wayne
was just standing there in the room
with his daddy
Shirley went over and poured
two glasses of bootleg whiskey
he'd confisgated out sez you want a drink?
Tommy Wayne sed yas, I do, I think
and they did
then Shirley Clayborn sez
boy, do you know what's worst
than doing what you did to that girl
in the backseat of my Chevrolet car?
and he sez no Daddy, what?
Shirley Clayborn sed
not doing that to that girl
in the backseat of my Chevrolet car
and that's pain.
All my life I've had to known
I never had a daddy like that
and it aint no way I know how
to be one either
and you caint tell me you hurt worst
than I do about that

and besides
I busted my back up
like yours
and I think mine's worst
when I got home
I couldn't set up in bed by myself
so LaVerne put a screw in the ceiling
we hooked up a comealong
to help me get up and a belt
around my chest
so I needed to pee and I hit that ratchet

belt slipped down around my belly
I done comealong my back
up off the bed
I holler and here comes LaVerne
she don't know how to undo
that ratchet and let me down
she hit it three licks
there I am my head and feet
touching the bed and the rest of me
pretending to be a rainbow
with slipped disks
me needing to pee
the only way she could think of
to get me down so I'd quit hollering
was with a hacksaw
neighbors a mile off
heard me and come down fore
she got me cut aloost
seen where I couldn't help it
peed all over my bed
I couldn't do nothing but
lay in it

so don't tell me about the worst pain
cause it aint never the worse
it's always something better'n that
you can bet on it any day
besides here come the fatnurse
with her bedpan
so you better be getting ready, now.

EVENING

No rest for the wicked
and the righteous don't need any

That's done up right and through
let's go have a coldbeer inside
and set on the furniture

No, John, I'm going home
I'm tired, I'm going to bed
and I may not get up tomorrow
I may sleep all day

Oh no you caint do that
the auction starts at nine
they do weinerpigs first
we got to be there

I'll call you early at six
so you can sleep till then
we gotta have breakfast
and go to the auction

so you take and go on home
I'll be by to get you
in my truck
we got work to do
we gone buy us some pigs
make us some money
starting tomorrow morning

MY TOWN

PRELUDE

> You can't go home again
> > —T. Wolfe

> That's shit
> > —Bill Holm

Who said that?
did somebody say that
or was it one of them damn books you read?

It don't matter
it's a pile of crap
I go home every day
don't matter where I am
I'm the prodigal son coming back
I don't even need a Greyhound bus
I can go to my town right now
right here talking to you
because this
is everywhere
I've ever been

UGLY

Ugliest man in town
was Raphael Martinez
he's kin to them Martinezes
I never told you about
had them triplet boys
2 born hooked together on one leg
and this sister
that grown a extra tit
right above her hip they sed
but they never cut them apart
borned dead
so they took the 2
and put them in a museum
in a jar where you
can go to see them
looking at you through the alcohol
he wasn't born that way

herded sheep up above Sawmill Road
this one morning he woke up
wished he hadn't of
couldn't stand up the pain was so bad
he known he couldn't live with it
and it was too far to town
like a weasel inside him
chewing he said
he found his pistol
put it in his mouth and pulled
bullet torn out his cheekbone
shot off half his ear
never hit no brains at all
and that was the only bullet left
he couldn't get to the rifle

so after he waited to die
and finally didn't
taken his knife

cut his throat but didn't hit a vein
stabbed hisself but the blade
was turned wrong
on a rib and bounced off
stabbed hisself higher and harder
hit his collarbone so it broke
the knifeblade off
part of it stuck in the bone
he thrown hisself in the fire

sed that hurt too bad to stay
it was coals from last night
melted his face on one part
burnt off the hair on that side
where it never did grown back
closed up one eye
carterized his neck
where he cut it so it almost stopped bleeding
sed he could hear hisself frying
for somebody's breakfast
but he had to roll out
couldn't stand it no more
found a shoeing hammer
took and hit hisself
hard as he could
between the eyes
with both hands on the handle
knocked him out so hard
he should of starved to death
before he woke up
but didn't
had a lump the size
of a ostrich egg growing on his face
so he had one more idea

tied a pigging rope on his feet
drug hisself to this mule he had
a mean kicking bastard
crawlt up on his back

and tied his hands to his feet
under that mule's belly
sed he never known how that mule
let him get on he's hollering so
of the pain when he moved
that mule hated being loaded
and he'd even untied him first
he could of run off or kicked him
in the mouth there on his knees
he figgered that mule
would of at least thrown him off
over his butt and kick loose
cave mebbe the rest of his head in
mule turnt and went to town

got him there by afternoon
passed out
people who found him was ascairt to death
seen that one side
didn't have no face left
blood all over that mule
like he'd been swatting flies on him
with a icepick
they took him to the hospital
couldn't figure out what was wrong
saw all them holes in him
burnt-off spots
blood everwhere
when they went
to lay him out straight he'd scream
like hell and they couldn't understand
a word of it
the only English he's speaking
was Spanish
couldn't wake him up enough
to shift his gear
tried to patch him up
best they could
without it costing much
they known it wasn't no insurance

nobody wanted the mule
that night they sed
he set up hollering like a sonofabitch
grapt his privates like
he'd pull it off
they taken and given him a shot
by next morning
he passed as big as the end of your thumb
this kidney stone
sed it turnt his pecker inside out
never seen one that big before
he bored a hole in it
worn it for a necklace
I seen it many a time
my god he's ugly
about half a face
with the eye shut on that side
half a ear
throat cut scar and his arms
blistered from his elbows to hands
where he lain in that fire
dent between his eyes
and a big white spot
where his cheekbone used to be
before the bullet come out
wasn't a kid in town
who'd stay on the same side of the street
as he's walking on
never bothered him a bit
he's happy as a goose
and about that many brains left

so about a year before he died
he come in to the doctor again
all wadded up in a bunch
his kinfolk brought him
give him the examination
and the X ray by then
doctor sez I got bad news for you

sed his face went as white
as a Nazarene preacher or a highway patrol
doctor sez you got the cancer
Raphael Martinez almost fell off the chair

started laughing and bawling
did the cross thing
sed oh thank god goddam thank god
I's afraid it'd be the kidney stone again
he's so happy they sed
it almost looked like that face
would of busted like a balloon
sed he wasn't afraid of no cancer
or dying cause he'd been there before
but with the kidney stone
it wasn't no way he could find out
how to not be there when it happened
and that's just too ugly
for him to have to think about

PREACHER

In 1956 Babtists got a new preacher
Reverent Pastor Brother Strayhan
from the Southern Tennessee preacher school seminary
he had a Bible they give him
for graduating had about 40 ribbons
marking his page number
hanging out the back
every color you could imagine
after he'd been there about a year
still tell them about how
they didn't appreciate him enough
because he was awarded them ribbons
for being outstanding in his field
one day Mizrez Bouchier
who was old enough to not care no more
sed after church she wished
he'd go back and stand
out in his field some more
she had enuf of him arredy

he'd preach swinging that thing
round like a Chinerman's kite
by the end the sermon
he'd took out the ribbons marking spots
all worked up to give the invitation
swung it so hard oncet
them ribbons chopped the top
off a incarnation in the pulpit flowerpot

he loved to preach on how
he got calt by the Lard to be his servant
when he's only 16 years old
met his lovely wife that same summer
my mama sez she figgered he's right
all boys that age get calt
some of them even on the telephone

but she thought the Lard
got a wrong number that time
we all scrut up now and then

he had about 9 kids
sed it was the Lard's will
oldest one not even 12
his wife looked like a inner tube
without about half its air
you'd hear her in the grocery store
2 aisles over
her feet drug so
she's wore out not even 30
and known it was her
before you saw her
by the sound

even if he got his preacher pay
and a house and a car
and his electric and water
with all them kids he thought
it wasn't enough to get by on
every 3d Sunday the sermon
was on the collection plate
and the bread on the water
he'd go round town
asking all the businesses for a preacher discount
wouldn't buy nothing in a store
if they didn't mark it down for him
when they didn't
he could make them sorry for it
he'd find some way to get it
into one of his sermons
whole churchhouse would go
somewheres else after that
whether they believed it or not
his kids got in the pitchershow
half price and free meals
at the school lunchroom
and the ball games without paying

because it was the Lard's will
so oncet he went to Lela's cafe
for supper with his whole family
stood there at the counter
before he'd set down
sed how much is your menstral discount
to eat there
customers listening 2 waiting to pay
sez I need at least 20 percent?
Lela sed whar? she wasn't even
a Babtist but a Presbyter
sez my family and I get discounts
because of I'm the Babtist Reverent
of up to half at most places
one of the people eating there
Clovis Robinson I think
sed yes ma'am that's a fact
he's a Babtist deacon
had to back him up without no choice
wasn't nothing she could do
everbody watching to see
if they'd all walk out
Lela sed set down
I'll do my 20 percent one time
all them kids standing there
with their mouths hanging open
3 of them didn't even
have their britches zipped up

he ordered tunafish sandwiches
and a glass of water
for all them kids because it was cheapest
fried chicken for his wife
because that was most for the money
and told the waitress
to bring him a steak to eat
how do you want that cooked? she sed
Scriptural he sed
she sed what?

he sez well done
my good and faithful servant
leant back and grint
proud of hisself like he thought
she ought to brang him a dish of icecream
for free for thinking that up

Lela heard it
hollered through the window
from the cash register to the cook
whole cafe listening
fix that preacher's kids hamburgers
with french fries
make his wife shrimps and whitefish
put him a steak on
from off the bottom of the pile
I'll pay the different
cook sez how he want that steak?
she yelled Scriptural
burn that sonofabitch to hell
he never did come back there
to eat again after that
and it never hurt Lela's business
not even one bit

Lazy

Laziest man ever was Floyd Scott
it wasn't nothing that boy
would ever do for anybody
when he's 5 years old
arredy too late his mama one day
sez Floyd come take this trash out
to the barrel but he just lain there
in the living room on the furniture
so she sez you taking this trash out
like I told you?
he never answered she sed
you want to take this trash out
to the barrel or do you want a whupping?
he sez finally how many licks?
she sed 3 with the flyswatter
he didn't say nothing for a minute
she thought he's coming to get it
then he sed do I have to
come out there or will you come
give it to me in here?

When he's about 12
they had supper one night called him
to come set down at the table to eat
he sed he wasn't hungry yet
they sed you don't have to eat then
he sed he was arredy there
he might as well wait till he felt like it
set there 3 hours with his elbows
on the table waiting to get hungry
they hadn't put their windowscreens
up yet and it was hot, windows open
his mama come to check on him
his face swolt up like a pomegranate
mosquitoes eat him up
couldn't even closed his mouth

had 3 mosquito bites on his tongue
too lazy to get up and move
he sed it was their fault
he calt for somebody to come close that winder
they had the television up so loud
he couldn't holler above it
it wasn't polite to get up
from the table before he's through eating

got him a job with his in-laws
where they couldn't fire him cause he's family
he wasn't worth a damn
tried to get him to string fencewore
left him there one morning
they come back to get him for dinner
he's still standing there with his hands
in his pockets staring at that wore
come up and touch him on the shoulder
he jumped straight up with his eyes open
sez goddam you snuck up on me
when I's studying how to unroll
all that wore out straight for 4 hours
give him a shovel to dig with
he leaned on it till he had a dent under his chin
had to go to the doctor to see
if the bottom of his tongue ruptured
for years when they wanted a shovel
they'd say bring me Floyd's dragline here
had to promote him to a desk job
for setting a bad influence on the other hired hands
give him the job of making coffee and answering telephone
he wouldn't even do that
his mama'd bring him to work and make it for him
had to buy a answering machine
he sed every time it rung he was always
busy checking the coffee or setting in the toilet

he was 24 years old when he
went and got in the car to drive

down to the grocery store a block away
to get him a can of beer
had this terrible itch that was a tragedy
he stretched up to scratch his ast
hit the curb and rolled the car
on flat ground right over
Doctor sed he couldn't find
nothing wrong with the X ray
but his back wasn't strong enough
for him to walk on it after that
insurance bought him 4 different wheelchairs
all too hard for him to use
till they got one with a electric motor on it
he sed he was satisfied
never walked a hundred steps in a row after that
some days he sed it was too hard and not worth the effort
to even get out of bed to it
so he got a television set in his bedroom
to help him get by on social security
that same year 4 kinds of welfare
and the Assembly of God brought his supper
on all days with an R in them
county paid for him a private nurse
because he sed it was a soft spot
in that pavement caused his accident
of their negligence and behavior
he was gone sue the county
and the town for a million dollars
if they didn't take care of him till he got well
they thought it'd be cheaper to buy him a nurse
for however long it took
after 3 years she found a way to get married to him
and still have the county pay her for being a nurse's helper
bought them a trailerhouse they put in
right next to his daddy's house
where he didn't have to pay no rent
after that she give up her other patients
and kept the county money for watching him
it was enough to get by on they sed

she's almost as lazy as he was
I heard moss grown in her toilets
they put a deep freezer out on the front porch
to hold the TV dinners she fixed
on all days without an R
both of them got so fat they had to have 2 couches
in the living room to set and watch TV on
so lazy a dog couldn't live with them
it'd of starved to death waiting
for one of them to come feed it

INTERLUDE

Help me right here sed John
and I grasped the bottom rim,
we lifted the barrel into the pickup
then sat on the tailgate, hot,
a warm canyon breeze
spilled across the yellow grass

It was this one summer back home
I's young about the time most kids
getting out of school
but I'd done quit
old man Cummings
had me helping him lifting all this heavy weight
on a wagon load
we made a tote and set in the shade to rest
he must of started remembering
commenced to talking sez
summer clover jingle jangle

he done taken and put his hand
in his pocket and pulled out this silver dollar
looked at it like he never seen it before
smooth so you couldn't even tell
the man on the side, all the words
rubbed off from being carried so long
it was meadow clover all over
stretching out green and yellow
I didn't say nothing, he talked, sed
I was 17 they come in wagons
putting on Gypsy carnivals
whole town wanted them to go on
known they'd steal whatall's loose
everbody went to the tent that night anyway
they paid me a dollar to water horses
I worked all afternoon hard
I was 17 for a dollar

she had eyes that laughed
same color as them fancy shoes
laugh like silver bobbles
on a red-and-blue velvet dress
color of midnight
even in the dark I seen me
looking back from those black eyes
I wasn't scared
she shown me slow, easy
the whole field of yellow clover
bells on her shoes real soft
jingle jangle

so many nights I can't sleep
smell comes in the window after me
when my wife's alive times
I lain the whole night beside her shaking
awake, all that dark
tearing holes in me
nothing I could do but stay there
listen for the sound of silver windbells
kids in the next room, sleeping,
nobody could smell it or hear it but me
summer clover jingle jangle

he set there staring at that money
in his hand
almost like he's talking to it
like he done forgotten
I was there too
never sed no more
put it in his pocket
and closed his eyes
I could tell he's smelling the summer grass
it was all over for then

so let's take this pigfeed
out to the pens and we'll be done
lifting it down won't be as hard
as getting it in
2nd half's always easier'n first

George Landrum was called Goosey
in town because he was
and when he got married they had this baby
that inherited everything from him
that baby grown up the same way
he was Little Goose in town
him and this womern had this baby
they named George which was my friend
before she run off to Oklahoma with a Indin well digger
his daddy was a Campbellite
didn't believe in no divorce or piano music
he waited for her to come back some day
but it was too late and she finally didn't
what they called him then was Poor Goose
he's ruint all over town
they'd all pray for him with the sick and afflicted
even the Lard known who Poor Goose was
but she was gone for good

before that
before they dug all them dry holes on their place
before Goosey the granddaddy hung and killed hisself
after his wife took off when Poor Goose grown up
even before he got behind on the taxes
and lost part of their farm and Kay Stokes picked it up
somebody give the grandboy they called Baby George
these 2 gooses for a birthday present
to be funny about it all
but he raised them for pets around the house
so one day eating supper they seen
them 2 going off down the road through the gate
Poor Goose sed there they go
you better get them back inside the fence
and close that gate if you want to keep them
that boy run out to do it
in a minute they looked out the window

he had one goose under both his arms jumping up and down
they could hear him hollering through the wall
Leggo goose, leggo me goose
went out on the porch sed what's going on?
boy turnt round still jumping
both them long-necked gooses had leant over
and bit him on the pecker
he squoze so hard one passed out
they thought it was dead
its head down flopping like a well-bucket
and they'd have to eat it but it wasn't
othern hung on until his daddy
jerked it loose but it was a tragedy
that goose flopped its wings and given him
a bloody nose
and it broke that boy's pecker
must of busted something in there
turnt off to the east
almost like the letter L ruirnt
took him both hands to pee from then on
he never did get married by choice
sed he never had no inclinations or otherwise
it was too much pain for being married to be worth it

so after that
after all the wormen left and Goosey hung hisself
and Poor Goose and Goose Neck
which is what they called him at first cause it looked like one
was living alone out there together
for the rest of their lives
about to lose the whole farm during the drought
with no money coming in to nobody
before they noticed it them 2 gooses
turned in to over a hundred
you couldn't come up to their gate even
here all them gooses would run up
with their wings and tongues out
hissing and squawking like a oilwell fire
even the Jehovah Witnesses couldn't get up to their porch

they'd of busted your knees flopping their arms
then you'd slip on goose shit and fall down
they'd bite off all your private parts and ears
before you could crawl off and get away
and that saved the farm
is it a rag up there
I can wipe off this oil with?
no dammit not a clean one
one I can use on oil
you wearing a tee shirt?
take it off and give it here

M.L. Basinger come in
with the drilling and well supply
had his machinery and parts spread out
acrost his property
people started sneaking in and stealing it at night
dogs didn't help
they'd bring dead meat and feed them
walk around and take whatall they wanted
he's about to lose everything
when he heard about the Landrum geese
went out and offered them 5 dollars apiece
for as many as they'd sell him
made enough to pay the taxes
and keep the rest of the land
it stopped the stealing right now
bunch of field hands cut across Basinger's
one evening after work singing out loud
just got the gate close
there was all them geese
if they'd of kept singing it might of been all right
but they turnt round and went quiet
like something was the matter
that was what them gooses was looking for
it was like a bale of cotton busted in a hurricane
scairt them so bad they couldn't get that gate back open
tried to run but they couldn't get away
one fell down and about drowned hisself
on dry land holding his face in the dirt

so them geese wouldn't get his eyeballs and nose
tried to climb that fence with the rusty barbwore on top
cut their hands up like it got caught in a gin grinder
tore their britches almost off going over
one got tangled up and his foot stuck
hung him head down on the fence
but them geese couldn't get to him on the other side
his face a inch away
this one goose trying to get its head through the fence
hissed till he had goosespit down the side his mouth
screamed so loud they thought it was a firetruck
all in Spanish they couldn't understand a word of it
but them geese seemed to know what he wanted
made them so excited
you could hear it 4 miles away
had to cut him down with some pliers
they thought his ankle was busted
never found out
he hit on his head and come up running
none of them field hands said they didn't never
see him again he was gone
them geese chased him down the fence
trying to get to him heading straight south
they had them some plans worked out for him
M.L. Basinger after that put up a sign
sed KEEP OUT THIS PROPERTY IS PROTECTED
BY LANDRUM ATTACK GEESE
YOU COME THROUGH THIS GATE
YOU WILL PROBLEY DIE

it was such a good idear
everbody wanted to buy some of them geese
even Charley Baker for his junkyard
and tied that sonofabitch dog up with a chain
but somebody told them idiot kids of his
they could populate with a goose
so he had to let them go
but it was worth a try he said
that dog was too mean even for him
but it never bit them idiots even oncet

that's how the Landrums got by and
held on to their land selling geese
for all them years till they give it up
but now you know something most people don't
who lived here all their lives
they think them people was call Goose
because of what they raise
that's how come nobody can pass a history test no more
they don't know before from after
and most don't give a damn either way
just what's on television and have supper ready on time
which if you push too hard on when she aint in the mood
can get you in a lot of trouble
set the whole thing going all over again
like the way it works when you don't pay attention
sometimes your goose don't get cooked
you have to live with it
and that can last a real long time
get in and turn the crunk over
let's see if this sonofabitch'll start yet
we'll drive to town and buy something to eat
if you need supper that bad before it's ready

WILLIE AND THE WATER PIPE

> Then you have done a braver thing
> Than all the Worthies did
> —John Donne

Willie Dalton would have laughed
if he'd been there
for his own funeral
8 men carrying his box
any one could have
carried him off like a floursack
he never stood 5 foot tall
in cowboy boots or weighed
a hundred pounds a day in his life
his own family sed they thought
that doctor must have thrown out
the baby and got the other part
to breathe he's so runty

he's a horse jockey
didn't have much choice of it
broke 3-year-olds every spring
at all the ranches around
one time a man sed
in front of him it wasn't ever
no horse alive Willie Dalton
couldn't ride and he sed
that's a pile of crap
any horse could of throwed him off
on a day but he'd try
and get back on
it was some thrown him
right back off again on his ast
but he made good money at it
busted almost every bone
in his body and his privates
one time or the other

it was a 4th of July picnic
we had for the whole town
back then every year
had running and jumping
rassling in it
so Leon Bilberry this one year
whupped everybody that tried him
he sed it aint no man
in this town I caint kick his ast
them words never even hit ground
before Willie Dalton was at him
jumped right up on his head
wrapped him up with his arms
one leg around his neck and the other
under his armpit and elbow
hollering like a strangled bobcat
he'd pry something loose Willie
would grab him another way
couldn't shake him off
Leon sed it was like a octopus
had his testicles wrapped
around his head
finally he fell down
whichever way he rolled
Willie went the other riding him
like he's breaking a mule
kicked his sides so hard he thought
9 ribs were busted
it was only 2
till he gave up Willie sed
say calf rope he did
say I give he did
say I won't never rassle Willie Dalton
never again he did
on his mother's white butt her watching
anything to get him off of him
he wouldn't rassle nobody after that

but what Willie did
that nobody else in our town
ever done before or since
was clean out the water pipe

town water come from
the mountain 7 miles
for ditch water and 4 drinking
so one spring both pipes clogt up
they fixed the drinking by geography
went halfway down and cut
it was no water
so half of that back up
till they found the plug third cut
and got it out
but the ditch water was different
not plugged off just partly
couldn't get a full stream of pressure
they didn't know what to do
so at the town board meeting
Willie Dalton sed for 2 bottles of whiskey
I'll clean that pipe out
they shut off the water
from the dam and he climbed in
the next day crawled that pipe
7 miles downmountain
through a 16-inch hole by hisself
with a flashlight
breaking up the bumps
to the bottom with his body
all day
when they opened that headgate
there was 5 dumptruck loads of gravel
and rock come out of that pipe
he'd loosened up going through

he crawled that pipe
30 years every spring
by hisself for 2 bottles of whiskey

even after he had a cancer
like half a cantalope
hanging off his neck
his whole skin yellow as squash
almost ready to die
that last time he didn't come out
till after dark
only 4 people left waiting to see
some of the rest sed
he's dead we'll warsh him out
in the morning sometime
gave him his 2 bottles of whiskey
Roy Talbert sed you gone open them
we'll have a drink?
Willie sed bullshit
that's all

they were sitting on his mantle
the day he died a month later
not even opened
with a letter they read
sed if I'm dead you can open these
and all have a drink now on me
not one man in town
even Curley Larsen would
touch one of those bottles
I expect they're still setting there
and the water pipe sealed itself up
2 years later with mud and rock
they never could clean out
all the farmers had to go to wells
because Willie wasn't there no more
they had to find another way
to get by without him

POSTLUDE

1

It's at least 2 people who'll never forget
the day old man Cummings died
I heard he's about to give it up
so I went by to see whatall I could do
like everybody else who'd known him for all their lives
it was a whole roomful of people
already there first when I come
wasn't even no open furniture nowhere
so we stood up or set on the floor waiting
while the otherns rocked or clucked

then the Reverent Jackson shown up
Reverent William Robert Jackson Lard's servant
back when we's kids growing up
we never called him that
he went to preacher school and got his churchhouse
we didn't know him no more
him and his name both got put into the revised version
he stopped being one of us for then
come in that house and sed
Has Brother Cummings expired?
I didn't have no words to answer that
but Lucille Cummings who had been his in-law
back before his boy Eugene she married died in his pigpens
face down in the mud of a heart attackt
sed Nosir Reverent but it's close
he been in his coma for 3 days now trying
the Reverent sez Brethern
let us bow togethah for a word of prayah
held up his hand so the Lard would know to listen
never got to the end of the first line
telling god who it was talking
we heard old man Cummings
call through the door to him

sed Billy Bob would you come in here for a minute?
not very loud we barely heard it
just like we was still kids in the school
and Mizrez Pennington had took one of us
down to Mr. Cummings back then
for being a disruption of influence
sed Shut the door behind you please son
we never heard no more
it felt like a little wind
went through that house shivering
looking for a place to curl up and lain down
it was after that when I heard the bells

2

he wasn't in that room but a little bit
when the door come back open
you could see right then by looking
Billy Bob Jackson had been down to Mr. Cummings
he wasn't gone be no trouble no more
for at least a long time
some sworn his face shown like Moses
coming back from the mountain
but he could of been trying not to be crying
like people have to do when them things happen
he sed Mr. Cummings he's went on now

at first he wouldn't tell us no more
I don't think he ever did tell everthing
but he finally come round sez
He was whispering soft so I couldn't hardly hear—
but I known he known what he was being told
we could see that because he quit talking preacher talk
we could understand ever word in his mouth
even when he finally sed that prayer for all of us—
And then it was like he looked right past me
like it was otherns in that room besides me
he stopped whispering and looked where they were
then he sez Well hello

it's sure nice of you to come
I swear that room turned warm like summertime
you'd think you could smell clover hay in there
when I looked at him again he was smiling
I could tell he done gone and left

3

they all talked about it for days and years
we should of built him a statue
but those of us who'd of thought of it wasn't expensive people
so he's just buried instead
some sed it was his wife come for him that day
some sed his boy Eugene must of been there too
the elders and deacons sed it was Jesust for sure with angels
Billy Bob never sed nothing else about it
and neither did I
there wasn't nobody for me to tell
but when I close my eyes and think about it even now
I can hear that sound I heard back then
of some silver bells jinglejangling in the wind

COVENANTS

Psalm Written After Reading Cormac McCarthy and Taking a Three Hour Climb to the Top of Pine Valley Mountain

> Laughter is also a form of prayer
> —Kierkegaard

Right here, Lord,
tether me to my shadow
like a fat spavined mule
stuck sideways in tankmud
bawling for eternity

At midnight
when the stars slip their traces
and race the moon like wild horses
to their death in the darkness
let my hoarse song twine with the nightwind

May the bray
of today's laughter fall
like a pitchey topbranch from a tall yellow pine
straight down like winter sleet
to the mountain's bent and trembling knees

HOUSEDOGS

> Not louder shrieks to pitying heaven are cast
> When husbands, or when lapdogs breathe their last
> —Pope, *The Rape of the Lock*

Ollie McDougald when I set down
at the counter to have coffee sed
he didn't want to talk about it
I seen he's down in the mouth sez whar?
he sed it aint nothing to speak of
I let it go and watched
while he stirred his coffee without no sugar
or milk in it with his spoon studying
sed finally if it's any of your business
it's that goddam fycet
my brother-in-law by marriage taken
and given to my wife she name Sweetie
now that sonofabitch lives in the house
all day and at night in our bed
it's about ruirnt my whole life
marriage done shot to hell
and dogshit all over the yard
what am I posta do?
B.L. Wayburn running coffee and cash register
listening in sez it aint nothing
about all this I don't know
so you curious you just axe me

I been married 3 times had 9 dogs
2 of them in the house by 2 wormern
I'll tell you now free of charge
2 things you can set your watch to
and live a life by if you want
1st is a married wormern can only love a thing
if she can pity it and then run over it
which is why they let them things
set in their laps smelling them
watching TV in the house

whenever they scratch on the door to get in
and the 2nd is what your daddy
should of told you in high school that
a wormern's love is like morningdew
sparkles like a diamond in a goat's ast
it might land on a red garden rose or a turd
it won't known the difference
you better make yourself accustom
she ever has to choose between you
and that shiteater you just as well
get on down the gravelway kicking roadapples
one of them might be dew wet
remember it caint necessarily help it
her and it just likes the shine
so all you can do is scrape off your shoes
come on in and set down
try to outlive it and not get anothern
that dog's as permanent and official
as Judge Parker in his courthouse
you want to stay married
make you a compromise and do it her way
that's all there are to it

E. U. Washburn's Story: Uncle Abe

> I have not wasted my life
> —Richard Shelton, "Desert Water"

Genesis 17:7

1

Oncet when I was a boy
a walking man come
to town twicet every year
folks didn't know who he was
name him Uncle Abe
sed he was lost and wandering
in his own mind
a harmless old thing just passing by

carried this paper bag in his hand
no child or cat can not find out what's in
I sidled him in the gravel road sez
Mister Man, what you got in that paper sack?

he turnt round looked me up and down
like a rooster hypnotized
by a line in the sand
sed Master Boy, I'll tell you what I brought
but you answer me first one thing
you say how many years your mama's got
I told and he sed not enuf
tell me your grandmama's home
I sed she aint she's dead and gone

he say
    I was a almost whole live grown up boy oncet
    like you walking along soon
    had me a paper sack of store bought candy
    going down the road
    after work at the cotton gin

girlchild womern on her poach call me say
Mister Man, what you got in that possible sack?
come here show me right now
patted beside her where for me to set
I come to her she say what you bring?
I shook all over
she was beautiful as churchhouse sin
I felt as ugly as the real thing

she eat a piece without asking
I known deep in my paper sack it was
one chocolate covenant hiding to be last
pretty soon we almost racing
eating that candy so fast
she lay one smiling piece on her tongue
with her finger say come here
put her mouth on mine
she pass me that seed
take it back and again
till the covenant was gone
then so was she
all but the memory

I had me one wife, son,
four good chirren grown up
left and gone
but never nothing
like that day since come along
now I got hope and mebbe
and then whatall time's left
this paperbag of sweet candy
with one covenant
for her somewhere waiting
if I'm so blessed

3

he told me his story that day
again every time since twice a year
till the day he didn't come here

I never stopped remembering
the promise I made
to never have to say
I got no more of my life to waste
I still try to look
down every street
at every porch
every old walking man's face
every shadowed place

4

oncet Mama say
you don't be shiftless boy
don't you daydream your life away
pretty soon you be walking lonesome
empty head and pocket
like that crazy Uncle Aberham
kicking rocks down the gravel road

I sed oh Mama Mama
don't even promise that might be so
it's a whole live world
inside that lucky man
you and all the rest of this town
don't even know
one sweet covenant
you can't never understand

RHAPSODY FOR THE GOOD NIGHT
CHRISTMAS EVE '94

Matthew 8:22

1
Libations
liquid and flowing
beneath the knees of the gods

Strangest man ever was E. U. Washburn
his Bible name was Ethopian Eunuch
come from that family opened the book
whatall was there got named
had Cephas Peter that we called C. P. or Junior
and hated because he went to school studying typewriter
come back educated where he known
the meaning of life and wrote it in a 4 page paper
for the college
loved to tell about it but never got the idea
wasn't nobody listening
the other brother Phillip Chariot
we called Bubber because he had his harelip
so he watched television until Floyd Scott
got fired at Christenson's Brothers
they hired Bubber to make coffee and clean office
nurse tried to not let them name him that
but Dr. Tubbs sed go ahead
they'll call him by the letters anyway
they did so E. U. worked at the graveyard
digging and tending with Jesus Salinas

he's the baby so they raised him with Bubber
probley not talking a whole lot
when he's grown up most people or some
never known he could say nothing at all
some sed he was deaf and dumb
addled but they's wrong all 3 ways

he mostly didn't like to talk
he'd come to the cafe by hisself
set and listen and nod

oncet it wasn't no place open to be with people
I went back to where he was in the booth
sed E. U. can I set here with you drinking coffee?
looked at me but I never set down till he nod
sed how ya'll anyway? he lipped justfine
1st time I heard him say anything
when we through not saying nothing
for a 1/2 hour listening to the otherns
I sed I gotta go you need a ride?
I had to drive past the graveyard to the farm
he never sed nothing then either
got up paid his bill
went out got in my truck
both of us drove to work that way
for moren a year till I got a job
at the sawmill and had to leave early

he talk soft
couldn't play no radio to hear him
when he sed something at all

sed them's the hardest that day when I sez
it's bad about that Reuben Jimenez boy
who was in the Boy Scouts until he
died of the appendicitis when he's 14 in high school
on the operating table without waking up
it was a month later before he sed more
that was what opened the gate

sed that boy isn't figured out he's gone yet
I dunno what to do about it
they buriet him in the wrong place
isn't nobody there to help him or tell him what to do
I sez whar?
didn't have no idea what he's talking about

he sed that Jimenez boy
longest speech he'd sed up to then
I had to think for almost a week
couldn't make it add I sez
how do you know? then without asting what?
he sed I can tell

2
nightbird
and the hum of pickup tires
on hardscrabble

I listen
behind the mockingbird behind the wind
behind the sound a taproot makes
working its way down to water
past that I can hear them
theygn hear me too
if they want to
but they mostly don't
sometimes I talk
not to them mostly
to myself to the wind
to the field mouse under the plastic grass
in the shed by the mesquite tree
sometimes they pay attention
it's other ways too
like how they settle in to stay
or don't

Leona Huffington there
has her back to her husband
won't talk to him
but doesn't even know
he don't care

Baucis and Philemon Rojas had both
sed look for a bright spring sunrise they'd be
in bed sleeping in their morning garden

next to each other past tomorrow's dawn
Jesus thought the one plot was fine with the
headstone with one name but both in the one
red box under a blanket dressed that way
he wasn't sure of but they'd planned it through
it was what they wore their first night they wrote
so Rufus did just like they said then we
planted on both sides of their place the two
rose stalks they'd raised by their garden window
roses bloom now over the stone in a
bow bright red as Easter morning sunshine

that other rosebush over there by Tommy Malouf
it's growing right out the palm of his hand
and in that flowerplant it's a mockingbird
every day pointing itself right at
Janie Grace Gossett who got killed
in the car wreck in high school singing
aint never a weed grown at her place
that Malouf boy give her flowers and the song
she settled right in knowing she belonged
some out there's helpless
like that Reverent Brother Strayhan
found out it aint at all
like what he been told to think
now it's too late

biggest surprises
was Ellis Britton and Kay Stokes
everbody thought Ellis he wouldn't never
fit in cause he's so mean
he was the happiest I ever seen
found out we's all wrong
he never hated the people
he hated the living
Mistah Stokes now on the other hand
he hated us all
so he aint never settled in
probley won't

at least as long as Jesus is watching
can't get used to not being in charge
on a night of a full moon that comes on a payday
I seen Jesus out there with him getting drunk
telling him about all the times he come
thrown him and his family off the No Lazy S
sworn at him in front of his chirren and dog
now he sez Well now Mr. Kay Stokes I believe
I'll go fishing down to the tank by the blue gate
catch me that big catfish they say down there
so what you think about that Mr. Kay Stokes dead man?

I'll swear I seen
one thousand dandelion weeds pop up
all over that grave in a night
when he's been listening to Jesus
whole grave come up 3 inches
he's trying so hard to get out
I rakes him back down in the morning sunshine

Ellis Britton settled
in 2 weeks or a month
so fast we never paid it mind
when the otherns out there saw he's ready
they started the rumor
we all have to come back do it again
he slunk down deep and low as he could
holding on tight
took 2 wheelbarrows to level him up
he just fine
a satisfied mind

3
Music is silence.
The reason we have the notes
is to emphasize the silence.
　　　　　　—Dizzy Gillespie

owl say who
preacher say whar
Rufus say here
me and Jesus
we start building
a hole in the ground
he sing
Lead me gently home father
dying
crying
singing
preaching
praying
bringing
burying

then we all begin
the next beginning
covering
forgetting
remembering
calling
neglecting
loving
hating
moving on along

out here
back there
all the same:
wind blow
bird sing
grass grow
churchbell ring

nightime quiet
it all sink in

4

romantic interlude
of a windy afternoon:
sunlight and elmshadow on stone

year later Christmastime
I seen E. U. of a morning sed set down
we drank coffee till the otherns left
he sed I got that Jimenez boy settled
I sez you did? he sed yas
but it almost costed me the farm

wasn't nobody heping
they done forgot about him
all alone and ascairt
down there whar it aint no time
I had to extablish a reason
they had to hep him in

I known if I could get Mistah Kay Stokes
working against my case
they'd all the rest hep that boy
I sed aint we all from the same clay?
he sed mebbe that's so boy
but it aint no jug is a vase

I sed does a man
have to come down there early
to set that boy to rest at home
cause if you aint gone do it
then I'll have to
Jesus'll clean your yard alone

That's whatall it took
Ruby Patrick sed to her own daddy
neither one's porcelain so there you go
Janie Grace Gossett sed whar's that boy?
Tommy Malouf sed I'll find him
mockingbird flown to the Rojas rose

it was a whispering in the grass
in the trees in the wind whar? sed Ellis
whar's he at whar's he at they sed donde donde
mockingbird took him the song
in words he could understand
in a day the prodigal son he come home

5

in his hand a glass
filled with the moon
      drowned in branchwater
or
what E.U. said
on Christmas Day

here's to the newyear
and here's to the old one
and here's to the place in between
the sunrise and the morning
between the midnight and the fullmoon
that place
between the owlcall and the mockingbird
between the roostercrow and the last henlight
under the trees under the rose
under the grass under the shadow of a footprint
that place
where all the naming and the doing
where all the listening and talking
where all the lying and the truesaying
where all the storying and the singing
where all the words theyselves
which is the first and last thing of all
slide into quiet
that dark sleeping place they can call home
just between the dreamsay
and the realsay of it all
that place
where those who know
who live there

know that without the making and remembering and telling
to help us all get on along
it aint no difference or worth finally
in none of it at all

—for JoDee, with love

NEWS FROM DOWN TO THE CAFÉ

The Fish

> ... victory filled up ..
> from the pool of bilge
> where oil had spread a rainbow ...
> ... until everything
> was rainbow, rainbow, rainbow!
> —Elizabeth Bishop, "The Fish"

Arty Gill went down
to the cafe that Saturday morning
to have coffee with the boys and that's all
until he found Cephas Bilberry and Roy Talbert
ready to go fishing and he knew
that's what he wanted to do too more than life
even bought an extra case of Lucky Lager
so they could make sure
they all had good times
he was as happy as a goose
that found him a half pound of raw bacon
his wife Modean had to call B. L. Wayburn
at 10:12 that morning waiting long enough
for him to get done and back home for chores
to find out where he was
didn't even come home to change his clothes
only thing she'd told him he had to do
that day was fix the shelves in the closet
and clean out the storage shed
so she could get to the canning jars
with maybe one or two other odd jobs needed doing
he was going to hear about it
when he got back for sure
B. L. Wayburn sed he expected that to be a fact

didn't get home till after dark
all three chasing beer with whiskey
thirty-two fish in two towsacks
a pound or better one catfish
upwards of six to eight they bet

poured them all in the kitchen sink
went to the living room
sat down on the furniture to tell each other
how it had been catching them fish
one more time till they all three
went to sleep sitting up in their chairs
except Arty laying on the long divan
Modean never even came out
of the bedroom to look at the fish

woke up about three in the morning
to pee bad all that beer moving
Roy Talbert in the bathroom
being sick with the door locked
Arty couldn't wait he went to the sink
there was all those fish
his wife hadn't even
cleaned up yet he sed
the smell of it almost turnt his stomach
made him so mad he's ready
to knock down that bedroom door
make her get up and do those fish right then
had to hold them apart with his hands
all sticky and smelly so he
could see to hit the drainhole
if he hadn't been so dizzy from the whiskey
he'd of brought it all to an end
right then he had to lay down
room was circling him bad
when he got up Sunday morning
bedroom door still shut
he could tell she'd come out
about had a brain spasm when he saw
that trashy womern had made her breakfast
piled the dirty dishes after eating
right on top of all them fish
laying goggle-eyed waiting to be cleaned

he had it he went right to that door
sed Modean you in there?
jiggled the knob to see it was locked up
sed You come out here right now
get this kitchen all cleaned up
you beginning to embarrass me
saw Cephas and Roy Talbert staring at him
waiting for her to come put coffee on
sed Come on out of there Modean
wasn't no sound from that door
smacked his hand on it flat sed
You get on out here right now
get these goddam fish and dishes out
of this dirty sink and in the frigerator
you listening to me?
still wasn't no sound sed
You testing my patience I'm warning you

she sed then from inside the room
I'm not touching them fish Arthur
you can do whatever you and them two men
sleeping in there with you drunk
want to with them they're yours
he sed You say what? hollering by then
sed You heard me
I'm not coming out there till
you got that kitchen all cleaned
like it was when you come home
forty-two minutes after eleven o'clock last night drunk
he said Modean it aint my job
cleaning no kitchen with your dishes
I never messed up you come out that door
she wasn't talking by then
went in set down staring back
at Cephas and Roy Talbert
neither one offering any advice for once
just wanted coffee like it was supposed to be
hollered finally They'll lay there
a week before I'll touch them

real low they heard her say Fine
he said Two weeks by god
real low again she said
You drinking up your prime water
made him mad as a wagon
to be talked to that way in front of his friends
whether they's drunk or not didn't matter
jumped up and run to that door
smacked it with his fist screeching
like a hog being nose-ringed
You open this goddam door right now
I'm gone bust it off its hinges
stepped back and lowered his shoulder
bunched up to butt it down

door might as well of been invisible
or made out of glass
they heard the bolt slide open
sound of a shotgun shell
pushed in the breech
then the bolt close
like it was right there
in front of all six eyes open not blinking
Arty on one foot getting ready
to rooster fight that door froze in ice
Cephas and Roy Talbert putrefied
on the front of their chairs
then like an icicle melting come back
set that foot down
turned his head back at them
sed I believe she's ascairt enough
maybe I better let off the pressure
they both sed they believed
he was exactly right
wasn't no use to even talk about it
they better get on home now it's late
went out the front door
without even dividing up the fish

sed he couldn't stand it in there no more
all that cold air and dead fish
put on his hat and went
to the cafe for his coffee
wouldn't even talk to nobody about it
because they hadn't found out yet
when he got home she was gone

pushed him one too far he sed
made him some breakfast and thrown
his dishes in there with hers
on top of them fish in the sink
then dinner and supper when she
wasn't back from running off yet
including bologna rinds and bread crusts
he put water on so they'd stay soggy
slept on the furniture by himself
so when she snuck in late she'd see
he wouldn't sleep in that bed
with or without her by god
it was a matter of principle

third morning he got up looked at that sink
flooding over with dishes and garbage and fish
got so mad he stood there and hollered
at her by name for ten minutes
then run to that sink started throwing
everything in it out on the floor
fish stiff and crooked
all but one he couldn't believe it
that big catfish on bottom still alive
buried under there waiting
its mouth going open and shut gasping
for clean air as much as he was
thrown it on the floor and watched it flop
walked out the door and went to the cafe
had to sit by himself at the counter
had the fish smell too bad in his clothes
even Tommy Minor had a hard time

walking by him didn't even
hide that it was a task worth wages
Arty walked a path around them fish
all the rest of the week stinking
had to open all the windows
to let air in and out

drove to Tahoka on Sunday
to see if she might be over there
let her apologize if she'd had enough
nobody had heard of her they sed
Monday he couldn't take it any more
went in to look at the fish
saw them flybloat and oily
thought he'd proved his point
it was almost a week and a half
studied for an hour in the door
called Huffman Furniture to see
if it was any way they could come out
lay a sheet of linoleum over the top
mash it all down in between
Victor sed he'd send Ardell down
next morning but when he come he sed No
wasn't no way that'd work
he'd have to get it all up first
Arty sed what would he take to do it?
Ardell sed he didn't need no money
that bad yet he'd have to pass

Arty called every housecleaner in town
starting off with Juanita Valdez that day
they all sed no they wouldn't
word got out most wouldn't even
talk to him on the phone sed
they wasn't home and wouldn't be
for a long time more like his wife sed
he was on his own

must of urped upwards of a dozen times
during them latter days
where he wasn't lying any more
when he called in sick to work
they seemed to know it
come to the cafe they wouldn't ask
just bring him thin soup and coffee
at the end of the counter
with the door open for the air
even Roy Talbert didn't set with him
we wouldn't of thought he'd of noticed

Friday went with a grain shovel
and a sheetrocker's gas mask on his face
in that kitchen with the house opened
scraped up everything hadn't melted in
the floor and thrown it to his pickup
in a barrel so rotten it ruint it where
you couldn't even haul pigfeed
drove it out to the dump ground
where they made him pay four dollars
to unload in the dead-animal pit
and then told him he
couldn't even leave the barrel there
had to crawl back in and pour it out
haul it over to the landfill
so they could cover and bury it up

went home poured coal oil and turpentine
ammonia and Turtle Wax mixed with fly spray
on that floor until it looked like gravy
washed it out the door with a water hose
did it again twicet more
sed if it didn't get it out that last time
he was ready to burn it down
with or without no insurance
warshed up all the dishes he hadn't ruint
took all his smelly clothes
to Isaacson's laundromat and gave that girl

six dollars to run them through
as many times as it took
to get all the fish smell out with Clorox
went home and took a hot bath
with half a bottle of shampoo
four squirts of Wildroot hairoil and a bottle
of lemon juice with Babo stirred in the water
to get it out of his system

at the cafe they all sed
he looked to be a new man
let him have his coffee in the booths
with the real people up front
he sed he couldn't eat yet and it might be
a long time before him and his appetite
could get back on speaking terms
he was just glad to be alive and
he'd never again wonder how
it might be to live with Wesley Stevens
or be one of the Bullards

come home he couldn't believe
if it was a vision or the devil
Modean in the kitchen standing by the stove
cooking supper in fried grease on top
sed his knees went loose and he retched
out loud at the thought of fish frying
or being cooked in there in any fashion
she sed Warsh up if you gone eat supper
he couldn't take no more suspense
or tragedy in his life that day
held his breath and leant in to see
beans in a pot and fried potatoes
in a pan and a cut-up
chicken in that boiling grease
it was almost enough to make him
think he could ever be in love
with a womern like her again
changed his mind on the spot

didn't make her apologize
in public of her misbehavior and negligence
sed it wasn't worth it
it was all water under the boat in the past
he'd learnt a lesson to be learned
never again would he ever
bring home that many fish
to set in the sink more than one night
before he'd find a way
to get the neighbors to take some
even if he had to pay them to do it
and trying to find something like that
to get out of cleaning the storage shed
wasn't no way worth a new $200 kitchen floor
to save what's left of his
not very good in the first place marriage
sometimes it's best to not fish or cut bait
but just get the chores all the hell over with

A Hymn for Pearl

A day none of us who were there
will ever forget was when
they buried Pearl Nance
who wanted more than any woman
who ever lived not to be one

from the time she was twelve
she was God's experiment in gravity
any part you would have thought
could stick out got too big
pointed straight down
even her neck was a broken swivel
where her head studied only sidewalk

wore men's britches and boots
snap-up-front shirts with W.B. Garrett brown
and fingernail file snuffmop in the pockets
she could hark and spit and curse and lean
into a pickup fender
never did get the rhythm
to make it seem recreational
wasn't nobody to fault her
for not making the effort

it was a Thursday oncet
she went behind the cafe counter
late for evening coffee with this pint
she brought down from Johnston still
poured half a filled cup brimful
sed Here Brother Coy
let me buy you coffee this one time
him setting in his booth alone
like the cormorant in the tree
in the garden of life
with a harpoon to shove into any words
he heard and thought fit to drag up

for one of his sermons he brooded on
as a responsible affliction for the Lord
to visit on each and all of his many enemies
him and the Lord shared
in their enthusiasm for the gospel

only thing he could think of to say was
Why thank you ma' am
us struck as dumb as Zacharias
our meditation on the wish for his death
interrupted for the moment
and then: Why this here coffee has some bite to it
and then: Is it any possibility of a refill?
to which:

Pearl sed Let me bring you
a fresh cup Brother Coy
and then a third
and lo
him who we known as so filled with hate
he'd rot fast when he died
so E. U. always had a hole dug and ready for
ahead of time just in case
began to smile
began he to even laugh
for the first time we knew of ever

no one there could have predicted
the Lord's hand would reach out
and touch that one
it was a terrible mystery to us all
but when he stood and embraced Pearl
with a Christian's brotherly kiss
when she brought the fourth
it was a lesson
to never underestimate the power of the Lord
or the goodness of fine whiskey

and then she sed
Brother Coy I am become singful
and he sed Let us make a joyful noise
before the Lord
and began a spate of hymns
that tested the endurance of all the gods

fourteen times B.L. Wayburn had to unlock
the cafe door so half the town
and all the regulars could come in
until four in the morning from page one
"Trust and Obey" of Christian Hymnal #2
to "How Great Thou Art" pasted on the backside cover
memorized by heart in four-part harmony
plus two others unknown to music
so R.B. and Ollie could join
all together singing flatout

even old George Albany come in
the front door for once with his tray
and perfect-pitch tenor we never known of
did the solo in "Lead Shining Light"
Pearl rising to the occasion with her obligato
"Out of the Ivory Palace" Coy bawled on
and admitted for the first time
she thought in a previous life
maybe she'd been one of them eunuchs
in that Viennie boys' choir
and how much she must of loved it
as something to look forward to

Coy leading "I Come to the Garden Alone"
from the top of the counter
in between every stanza saying One more time
to tell the Lord you really mean it
so hot in that cafe by then
Baby Jesus was wilting off the inside cover
of the hymnals in their racks
in their pews in their respective churchhouses

scattered across the dark streets of our town
joined together for the first time in song
the only time any of us who knew him
professed any love for that sad man
and then she died

took three days to decide
she'd never been inside a churchhouse oncet
since she was old enough to choose
it wouldn't be right to inflict
the ceremony on her then
we all came to the graveyard instead

so many people they had to stand on chairs
and almost all the preachers including Brother Coy
to see B.L. Wayburn speak the words
we all sed as testimony
over coffee he wrote down
how when he came to the part
she was the founder of the Thursday Night Choir
which only met that one time
it must have been the inspiration of the Lord
us all breaking out together at oncet
with "Just As I Am" flatout
every one of us there who known
could see with our eyes closed
her big chest swell up
knowing she wasn't no longer alone
till all those pearl snaps on her cowboy shirt
popped open one by one

Conversation Overheard from a Back Booth on a Tuesday

1

"That man sitting beside you
last night at the party
what a nice man he was."
"Oh, Mama. Mama that man
he loves me. I think a lot."
"Yes baby girl. Surely
I did know that."

2

When I was a girlchild
oncet and I was
when Daddy worked in the mine
he brought all his possibles
and responsibilities home on the porch
for us not to touch on a weekend
that the Good Lord made for pure pleasure

it was on a Friday passing
into Saturday morning
after him being away all week a miner
making dreamplay in their room
all that house breathing love
and a whole live grown-up man
walking in a part of my mind
I didn't think my mama
knew about either
in the night

I had to go out on the porch
alone with the memory image of him
in the midnight
a giant storm throbbing

all around and inside
so I had to sit down
on Daddy's box from the mine
I didn't find out until tomorrow
was dynamites for the blasting

it was a wonderful
terrible storm that summer night
whole sky and house filled
with fire and thunder from all the gods
my body drenched with rain and sweat
until my nightgown held on to me
like love itself

I sat alone
with the shadows after the storm walked on
breathing in all the rainwallowed hay
and the yard and Mama's roses
opened and shed across the garden
glistening in the dreamlight
the whole live world exploded
and brought back together
by what happens
to us all, baby girl,
in a storm
on a summer night

SONG E.U. WASHBURN HEARD WHILE
TENDING ROSES OVER THE GRAVE OF
PHILEMON AND BAUCIS ROJAS

1 Corinthians 13: 13

Amor, ch'a nullo amato amar perdona,
mi prese del costui piacer si forte,
che, come vedi, ancor non m' abbandona.
—Dante, Inferno, v, 103-105

Is it true that Love is God? she asked.
And he said Yes, oh yes, it is true, my love,
but you must remember
to try and never believe it that way.

And then do you believe? she asked.
And he said Yes, I believe beyond death
in believing, yes.
That faith one can never fully give up,
there will always be doubt.

You must also remember to hope
and that in our language to wait
and to hope are one.
Espera, querida, espera.

And then what should I hope for? she asked.
And he said With all your heart
you must hope
that Love will keep believing in you.
Have faith in that alone

for only then will the world
as we believe in it continue
and that is God
and that is enough.

Epilogue Scribbled on Four Napkins and One Line on the Palm of a Hand While Sitting in a Back Booth with E. U. Washburn

> The past increases by the diminution of the future,
> until by the consumption of the future all is past.
> —Saint Augustine, Confessions, XI

1

B. L. Wayburn loved to say
After all's sed and done
around here more gets sed than done,
and I've come to believe that's best

It's all gone fast
the season, the year, our lives
in a whirlwind with fire and rain from the gods
tearing up the gift of good earth
and the faster it went
the more we could see the only thing
that changed was us and the calendar
all the rest stayed pretty much the same

2

Reverend Strayhan's fat wife
got fungus in her navel
that turned rot before they could
find it and get down to it
she died from the outside in
Coy choked on a dayold jelly donut
for half off with free coffee so bad
he had a double hernia
prayer and the Lord couldn't heal
so he wore a jockey strap and a truss
until Dr. Tubbs gave him the indigent rate
to sew his rupture shut

after he agreed we shouldn't have to
listen about the injustice any more

J. L. Biggins died of the heart attack
and Arlis Jamerson had such a stroke
he can only sit in a wheelchair and drool
but B. L. Wayburn's boy got discharged
for the convenience of the army
in time to come back and take over
the cafe after B. L. and the widow Wheaton
cashed in on the farmhouse fire and sold
the front half of the place to Sonny Gosset
who drilled a well and planted alfalfa
and gave a ninety-nine-year lease on the back 160
to Williamson's Associates on speculation
for a subdivision and trailerhouse park
after the insurance money cleared
so they could get married and go
on a honeymoon to Paris,
Idaho to see his kinsfolk there
and if it was time enough left
pull that little camper trailerhouse all the way
down to Carlsbad Caverns, New Mexico
so he could see for himself
what it was like to have his whole body
down in a hole besides a coalmine
where he could be like Moses Pharaoh
and reach out and feel the dark as black
as the inside of the Bible

3

E. U. sed oncet
that he heard the voices
while he was mowing
out to Mr. Cummings' place sed
The slipperiest thing on earth is time
what's coming sneaks up slow and quiet
like glue drying or road tar melting
but the past slides out the back door

like wishes and prayers covered with White Rose Salve
and chased by banshees

4

We got our gospel at the shrine
of the Wayburne Pig
where I learned to love the good news
from those old men more than life

E. U. and I had one unspoken wish
to someday sit in a front booth
and let our words mingle with theirs
until one Christmas morning in the mirror

there were faces we almost didn't recognize
behind Tommy Minor at the coffeecounter
and in a stroke blinding as Paul's Damascus light
we saw the evidence of the miracle of time

We had become a part of what it is
that we wanted most to say and do
and while that may not be churchhouse heaven
for the likes of me and E. U.
for the time being
it'll more'n do

5

That's all they are to it

SO QUIETLY THE EARTH

Dawn Psalm, Pine Valley

1

While I was not watching
sunrise came with a ruby throat
and gold-flecked wings.

2

Blue
and a small wisp of cloud
above the dark pine.
A jaysquall
leaves a small bruise
on one corner
of sky.

3

Boiling coffee.
A blue enamel pot
nestled in warm coals
beside the cold
sliding water.
Sky so close
you fear
bumping your head.

4

A brown breaks surface
rising to wingshadow
drifting on the blue selvage
of pond.

5

Golden lace.
Sunrise pours slantwise
into clear water

through the blue spruce
the deep tangle of pine
and purled woodsmoke.

6

I turned
and the earth hushed.
While I leaned into silence
a morning too vast to fathom
filled with light.

7

Praise.

The Grand Staircase

Each person
Has one big theory to explain the universe
But it doesn't tell the whole story
And in the end it is what is outside him
That matters, to him and especially to us
Who have been given no help whatever
In decoding our own man-size quotient and must rely
On second-hand knowledge.

—John Ashbery

A vast and primeval inland sea.
Sand and debris washed from the highlands,
sediment on the slippery film
of ocean floor. Water
forcing its weight downward, lime
and silica cementing these particles
into a mass of living rock.
The earth trembled,

convulsed great stone to the edge
of sea. Rivers
dragged their waters over
dihedrals. Marshes and lakes.
Ancient tides. A winter eon
and silence of brackish water.
Summer and swampy pastures,
lumbering dinosaurs. Layer
piled on layer as rivers and tides
built deeper, dark veins
of shale and sandstone rising
from a limestone pedestal.

Water broke on bedrock.
New seas splashed the earth.
A thousand feet of blood rock
over the chocolate belts.
Winds turned,

prehensile, tore down
a western mountain, drowned
the fertile sea in an inundation
of sand. Dunes choked rivers,
shallow lakes. The great desert
piled two thousand feet,
a riser of stone.

And the sea returned.

A shallow re-invasion teemed
with shellfish, reptiles.
Bodies mixed with sand, leached
iron pigment from desert rock,
metamorphosed to a plane
of Carmel lime, solidified.
The land yawned,
toyed with sea.
Sandbanks and gravel covered
mud and silt. A drab winter
crossed horizon.
Under a long cloudless night
earth slumbered in gray dreams
until birds called the sky
and the land stirred. Sea
drained away. Mountains folded
with the waking, thrust heavenward.
Clear water in bowls of stone between.
Rivers drained from highlands

eroding fragile ribs, carrying
the mountains grain by grain
to inland lakes. A pink sediment
spread the earth.

The land rose. In a great arch
it swelled two miles above the belly
of sea. Rivers carried away rock strata,
dug into earth. And the land

broke, dividing into great pieces,
plateaus, etched by deep fault lines
where rock separated,
valleys and basins. Delineaments.
Rains fell. Seasons turned. Winds
came. The earth breathed.

Abandoned Cabin on the Clark Ranch: Solstice

> Here's a marvail's convenient
> place for our rehearsal.
> —Shakespeare, A Midsummer Night's Dream, 3.1.2-3

1

Dark slides back, pools under the iron bed frame,
the crumbling stove, lurks in exposed joists.
A nail of sharp light through a missing shingle
cockeyed in the afternoon sun
angles the room as it huddles beneath
a caving truss, ceiling and floor in abeyance.
From the small east window, darkness empties
into clear day and the distance of green canyon,
then Cedar Breaks, the pink and orange badlands.
In the center a gray table, groaning chairs:
the eye slowly fills the four corners of room.

2

So then: Peter Quince: architect, carpenter, divine.
And on this June day a lost piece of sun
transfixes this chamber; tonight a point
of moonlight sweeps the wood floor. But the dust
is not stirred. Within the carpentry
of this one-room mountain cabin
in this dream of a man at a table
in a yellow-walled boar's nest study in his house
sharing memory with wind, dust lies still
in the moonlit apartment of the forehead.

3

In the stage set of the mind
a gray table centered on the floor
delineates the chambers of Peter's cabin: kitchen,
bedroom, den, hallway, sharp north, falling south.
Beyond the cleavage of warping pine
the window frames canyon, gnarled Breaks,

a rising almost transparent moon,
and brilliant wall of blue sky, the rock
upon which this dream is built.

Aspen Pole Fence

The aspen poles crisscross, a zigzag line
slicing the dry belly of the meadow, five high
at one hundred twenty degree angles compounded.
Such waste in a pragmatic sense. Consider
materials: five aspen poles per section at, say,
twenty feet per pole. With angles, six sections builds
approximately eighty feet of fence, a net loss of two
sections, ten aspen poles. But the gained strength.
And durability. Chester said the old Horse Valley
fence stood seventy years, which means fifty, until
Forest Service knocked the east side down, let
Job Corps put up sheep mesh, which went over
in the second year's snow. And the aesthetics.
Gods. The beauty of a cross-pole fence in autumn.

But the trees. The beautiful aspen cut wholesale
for such a piece of geometry: five poles per section
when one pole equals one tree once living now
one pole. Chester said there are plenty of aspen
in the first place and in the second some things
have to be sacrificed in the name of progress
and in the third that land belongs to him. Which
means the trees. Unless they can find a way to leave.
Which is why he built that fence in the first place:
so things wouldn't be getting away. They're only
trash trees. You can't get rid of them when you try.

Why is it that for some things there is partial sacrifice,
while others are required to give up all? At night
I can believe shadows of aspen trees grope along the far side
of the fence. I have not gone to see. In autumn,
when aspen spread the earth gold, I can think
the gray skeleton sprawling across yellow grass
is a good thing, Chester's fat sheep mindlessly
following its confines from one corner to the next,
to water, and back out toward the fence.

A completion, a perfect holding pattern. Then
always I see its direction: the aspen grove flowing
down the west hill, a twisted gray arm stretching
out toward the glistening splash of autumn color.

Yovimpa Point

for my Father
—Job 17:13

A stiff, pine-scented wind. The tough
gnarled trees behind me creak and groan.
Swallows dart from the pink cliffs,
swoop over the escarpment and wheel
through the maze of orange hoodoos.
Three thousand square miles of high desert
fall into southern horizon, down the staircase
to the Coconino where the Kaibab Plateau
hides the great chasm. On the eastern
circumference, the dome of Navajo Mountain
under a hazy sky. Westward,
Mount Trumbull huddles low against the earth.

Through this space I stare into the eye
of time. The rocks I stand upon are young,
rugged, weathered only twenty million years.
A thousand feet beneath this crenation
bland gray cliffs mark one hundred fifty million years
and on the near horizon the deep hue
of vermilion rose upon the belted strata
two hundred million years past. All rest
on a base of limestone twenty-five million years
preceding even that.

A vast ocean. A marsh
where giant ferns nodded in the sun and
great reptiles slithered into extinction.
A sleeping desert. A young mountain, thrusting
against a moving sky. The earth opens
before me.

Today once again, an ancient voice
in the wind calls, the same question

repeated: *Where wast thou when I laid*
the foundations of the earth? Declare,
if thou hast understanding.
Even in my silence, as I hold my arms
close against my sides, shivering
before the probing gust,
I grow more and more sure of my answer.
Here, Lord. I am here. In the beginning,
even now, here. Hues of pink and gold
beneath massive white formations fall
to green basin and the brilliant red horizon.
Gods. A world of gods, at play before me.

Kaiparowits Plateau

> Deep in their roots all flowers keep the light
> —Theodore Roethke

Tonight an enormous corn moon, fecund
and glistening, slides through a slow sky
over Navajo Mountain. Such undulations
this light, gliding the flat crest
of Fifty Mile, pulsing at the knees of Smoky Mountain,
almost a shimmering tide on the basin floor.

How long since
it seeped through the Cretaceous forest
into the nodding miles of blossoms
flowing across a tropical plain?

Tonight the mesa slumbers.
It dreams moonlight, metamorphosed,
hidden in the secret declivities, dark and moist
hollows. Its ancient forest broods in black silence.
Between gray rocks, from a small crack
in the sandstone plateau, a milkweed thrusts out
its yellow shoot, tastes the nightwind.

WHILE WALKING

For Jon, ages 6 to 8, with love

I
3 John 4
The wind is happy today.
How do you know?
Listen. She's singing.

II
Revelation 12: 1-2
Are all songs happy?
No. Sometimes when the moon sings it's because she's sad.

III
1 Corinthians 14: 7
How do you know she's sad?
Haven't you heard her? Listen.

IV
Isaiah 10: 19
Do you think a tree cries when somebody cuts it down?
I don't know. Do you?
Yes.

V
Luke 18: 16
Do you think the rocks are listening to us?
I don't know. Do rocks hear?
The ones that are alive do.

VI
Job 29: 5
Are all the rocks alive?
No. But some of them are.

VII
Proverbs 23: 24
Do the stars sing?
Yes.
In which language?
They sing in every language. Even the ones we don't know.

VIII
Matthew 18: 4
Do the stars sing in the daytime?
Yes. They always sing.
They never sleep?
That's when they sing best, when it's invisible.

IX
1 John 4: 4
You have to listen hard.
At night?
All the time. It's not hard. It's just not easy, either.

X
Ecclesiastes 4: 13
You have to listen. All the time. Even when you're not.
I see.
That's right. You can listen that way, too.

XI
1 Corinthians 13: 11
Be careful on the mountain. You could fall.
Maybe it won't let me.
The mountain doesn't care if you fall or not.
How do you know that?

XII
Isaiah 11: 6
Are you ready to go home?
I thought that's where we are.

Requiem

More than a high-desert sun dog shimmering
above thin lines of the Canyonland's open throat
or the sift of October-flushed aspen
on a gnarled Pine Valley, Utah, morning.
More than the pink fleece of a lost primrose
bathed in twilight by a graveled roadside
or the shadow of a cornstalk petroglyph
leaning into its basalt winter.
Beyond words sliding from hollows of memory
that hold image and time in stone cups
is the yearning, the bending to morning,
the huddled ache that can never be soothed
by moonlight or spring rains or crimson oak,
only by tomorrow's sunrise.

IN A HOUSE MADE OF TIME

The True Story of Susan Birchfield, Deputys Thibodeaux and the Texas Rat Snake

1

Susan Birchfield said the move
actually went better
than she expected
even though it took 432 trips
between the old house
and the new one on Silk Stocking
9 calls to the bank
4 to the preacher
1 to the J. P.
3 to the Joseys to reborrow
their big truck and trailer
and 2 to the marriage counselor
Dennis said before he'd move again
he would burn the house down
and start over
with or without insurance

Monday morning
him back at work
her time to walk through
just look it over by herself
with a cup of coffee
she felt good about everything
almost to the point of forgiveness
said she only meant
to look through the window
not at it
but right on top
of the drapes sprawled
like a three tawned housebroken cat
the six-foot snake
proud to be an adopted
Birchfield family member--

she remembered saying out loud
I can live without that
said she did not spill
one drop of her coffee
on the carpet or table
set it down
turned and picked up the phone
called the Sheriff's Office

Sheila she said
I need some help here
at my new place
Sheila said Is it a disturbance, ma'am?
Susan said Yes I believe so
Ma'am is it an intruder? Sheila said
Susan said Oh yes I believe so
Are you in danger, ma'am? Sheila said
Susan said I might be
but not in an immediate manner
Sheila said Ma'am, I'll send
Deputy Sheriff Thibodeaux
as soon as I can find him
Susan said Start at the coffee counter
at Adolph's and ask Laurie if he's there
Sheila said Yes ma'am I'll do just that

2

Yes'm Deputy Sheriff Thibodeaux
said when Susan Birchfield
opened the door after he rang the bell
I understand you have a disturbant
on your premise
she said Yes I do
he said Ma'am I understand you
have a intruder here at you house
she said Yes I do
he said I be here
to be of assistant
what can I do to help, me?

she said You come right this way
took him in to the living room
pointed at the window

he looked through it hard
to find out where it was hiding
whatever it was
until she put her hand in front
pointed his face up
said it took about nine seconds
of looking to see what he was seeing
said Holy Mary Mother of Got
blessed be the fruit of the loom
on baby Jesust
pulled out his pistol
hollered You stay right there
don't you move
she yelled No no
put that gun up
don't you shoot that
in my house
said his eyes could have been milked
if you'd grabbed and pulled on them
he was ascairt
said It's a snick up there
she said Yes it is
can you get him down?
he said No ma'am
I shoot him off there for you, me
I don't touch no snick
it be dangerous

stood right there in that room
like Lot's wife
looked at that snake
sleeping on top of the drapes
for a long time
pointing his pistol at it
she telling him four times

Don't you shoot that gun
in here you hear me?
he said finally You got any telephone?
she said Yes of course
he said l needa use it
mebbe l call my cuddin
he been to Snick School
he know what to do
she dialed the number
while he held the phone
with one hand
pointed his pistol at the snake
with the other

said LeRoy you get in you truck
drive you self right down here
to new Birchfield place
on Silk Stocking
where you see
my patrol car park
bring you snick catcher
we got us a problem, Houston

3

Mizrez Houston,
Assistant Deputy Constable
LeRoy Thibodeaux certified
in snaik removal at you service
how can l hep you? hidy yall cuddin Jodean
Howdy doodey LeRoy said Deputy Thibodeaux
My name is Mrs Birchfield Susan said
LeRoy get in here and lookee
we got us a problem Deputy Thibodeaux said
you got you snickstick?
Right here said LeRoy
walked in past Mrs Birchfield
without being invited
into her living room

Jesust Thibodeaux
LeRoy said when he saw it
that's a damn water mosacin
I think yes
You think so? said Deputy Thibodeaux
Mebbe a dimentback I think mebbe
Aint got no rattlers I see
Could be a giant coppermouf
I dunno
it's one damn big snaik
I can see yes, me
mebbe one them amaconda
crawl up through the sewerpipe
bite wormens on the butt
set and stare up
through the toirlet said LeRoy
Where they come from?
said Deputy Thibodeaux
I think Brasil down south somewhere
they say said LeRoy
That's a long way off to come
to bite a womern on her butt
said Deputy Thibodeaux
That's why they crawl
through the pipe
come out and eat babies
at night and crawl back in
how come you got you gun
out point at me
coonass? said LeRoy

I shoot that sonofabigsnick
he come after me said Deputy Thibodeaux
Don't you shoot that gun
in my house said Susan
Only if he come offer to bite on me
said Deputy Thibodeaux
Not in the house she said

What you gone do
Mr snickman now?
said Deputy Thibodeaux
We got catch this snaik
put him in a bucket
with a lid on it said LeRoy
You got a bucket with a lid?
said Deputy Thibodeaux
No you? said LeRoy
Hell no what I need a bucket
with a lid on it for?
how come you call me
coonass you peckerhaid?
said Deputy Thibodeaux

You got a bucket
with a lid on it Mizrez Houston?
said LeRoy
My name is Mrs Birchfield and there's
a soap bucket with a lid
in the laundry room said Susan
Would you axe Mizrez Houston then
if we could borrower that bucket
for mebbe little while
catch this snaik? said LeRoy
I'll go get it said Susan
You shouldn't call me peckerhaid
talk that way in front
of the wormen
who wake heah said LeRoy

4

What we do now? said Deputy Thibodeaux
You take this snaik stick
put the catcher on that big snaik haid
pull him down and put him
right in the bucket
I put the lid on then
said LeRoy

You the snickman
been to snick school
you put the snickcatcher
on his head I hold the bucket
Deputy Thibodeaux said
Aint what I train to do
I train to put the lid
on the bucket
after you put him snaik
in the bucket yes said LeRoy
I aint traint catch no snick
said Deputy Thibodeaux
That aint part of my job no

Go head said LeRoy
aint no problem
big one easy to see
what you doing
put snaik catcher right up there
catch him behind haid
pull he down and put him
in the bucket
Hell no said Deputy Thibodeaux
I aint touch no snick

Here said Susan Birchfield
give it to me
lifted the snake stick
up to the curtains
slipped the loop
over the snake's head
pulled it down
off the drapes
to the floor
where it sprawled
like an overfed pig

Gotdam lookee that bump
in his belly he done et sumin

mebbe somebody's baby
said Deputy Thibodeaux
No aint that big said LeRoy
I think me mebbe somebody's
little dog mebbe cat yes
It's a mouse said Susan
It's not big enough to be a dog
I think you right ezactly
Mizrez Ma'am said LeRoy
You better get him in a bucket
before he wake up hongry again
hold he up and put him in

Got him haid in said LeRoy
Jodean you put that damn gun down
put him tail in the bucket
I put the lid on
Hell no said Deputy Thibodeaux
I told you oncet and twicet
I aint touch no snick
Not gone hurt you said LeRoy
She got his haid down Mizrez Birchhead
Mizrez Birchfield said Susan
Hell with haid said Deputy Thibodaux
I shoot him right here
in the bucket
Don't you shoot that snake
in my bucket in my house
said Susan You put that gun up
I aint touch no snick
said Deputy Thibodeaux
Here she said Hold the snake stick

gave it to Deputy Thibodeaux
in the hand without a pistol

picked up the snake's body
wound it like a rope coil
into the bucket

Put the lid on LeRoy
Deputy Thibodeaux said Put it on now
I caint LeRoy said
Snaik stick he's in the way
you got to get it off
Get it off? said Deputy Thibodeaux
Yeah you grab snaik's haid
and take it offen, you

Here, said Susan
hold still
I'll do it
You be careful now
Mizrez Houston
LeRoy said
You don't be letting
him bite you any
I won't said Susan
Would you please
get out of the way Deputy Thibodeaux
I got the lid all ready
said LeRoy
When you get him off
we'll be all done and finish
pretty soon now all right
Don't let him get away
said Deputy Thibodeaux

5

Here you bucket ma'am
said Deputy Thibodeaux
we done toin that snick aloose
like you said we do
Did you shoot that snake
Deputy Sheriff Thibodeaux?
Susan said
No ma'am
I couldn't hit him
with no pistol

he done gone off somewhere home
out in the wood by hisself

I want pologize for my cousin LeRoy
he sometime got
a filfymouf on him
he don't mean nothing by it
he tell me he tell you
tell Mizrez Houston herself
you better warsh this bucket
out real good
for Mizrez Birchwood
before you used it
it got a whole lot
of snickhaihr in it
Oh yes, I will do that
said Susan, indeed
Yes ma'am said Deputy Thibodaux
I suspicion you will
do that about ezactly

and then she said
so she could get it
exactly right in his own words
as he might of said it
Witout adieu or au revoir
he got in his patrol car
to went and left
the premise
to look for him
a hot cuppacoffee
and somebody to tell
all about his day
about the bigamuch one
he toined aloose
and let him get away

In a House Made of Time

Matthew 25:14-30

Lucille Bullard was the best
wailer in the history of our town
also the first professional mourner
any of us ever knew about
she had the talent as a natural inclination
said it was a gift from birth
but diligent research enhanced her performance
read the Bible on sackcloth and ashes
went to Boris Karloff and Vincent Price movies
to hear women scream over vampires and
butcher knives and Iron Maidens and being turned
into wax mannequins role modeling
so she could share their grief
with all her women friends and children

most of it she already had in stock
she'd sliced the first two joints
off her pointing finger in a sausage grinder
when she was nine and her mother
cauterized it with a curling iron
put a bandaid on
said she wasn't going to waste
four pounds of sausage looking
it was gone for good
she'd already lost all her front
bottom teeth and one on the top at the side
in a fight with Leland Newberry at grade school
over whose turn it was to slide
her hair splotchy from ringworm scars
and with her fleshy weight all dresses
looked Pillsbury flour sack homemades

she learned her best effect passed down
in a legacy from Ruby Rushing

who picked it up when her husband Ike died
shared it with her nephew Wheelis House
who taught it to her at no charge
when she asked how he made it happen
swelling up his face till it looked
like it might explode with veins throbbing
both eyes puffed closed to bright red slits
he showed her how to bawl
into a steaming hot wet washrag for fifteen minutes
to get the proper effect
done exactly right it would stick
up to three hours in public
she was willing to shake ashes
all over her if necessary
had the full repertoire of sound effects
crying to bawling to howling
to wailing at which she was world class
to shrieking like the sound of rusty barbed wire
that would draw banshees

tried it as an amateur at three different funerals
to test her sense of timing and volume
went to Rufus the undertaker at Mason's
offered services as a professional
best he could do at that stage was put her in
as an optional part of the first class gold package
starting at five dollars per memorial
thought she might be able to build up
income as her reputation spread
she might try the preachers
since it could wax into a crowd pleaser
fill up the seats with potential tithers

did some wailing work with Reverend Strayhorn
then the Presbyters and Nazarites
so well for Kay Stokes' funeral
Scotty Sampson at the graveyard
wrote her a check for twenty dollars to do
his when the time came up

said he wanted the full spectrum
since he hadn't been able to locate bagpipes
lived fourteen more years during which
she perfected her performance and visited
him in the hospital when he was doing final preparations
about the occasion told him
she needed ten more dollars for inflation
since he was rich enough to afford high style
they argued for an hour before the nurses
called Dr. Tubbs to come get her
she was scaring the rest of the patients
he gave her five dollars and the nurses put in
the other five to satisfy her to go home and wait
Scotty Sampson bowed up and wouldn't go another penny
he said It was a matter of principle
Dr. Tubbs and the nurses didn't care
Jim Carmin had already said in public
both of them two's level was half a bubble off plumb
as an established fact

before that in the middle of her rise to fame
she became a legend when Coy Stribling
called and offered her twelve dollars if she would come
to the Church of God of Holy and Divine Prophecy and
Revelation and work Bill Gill's funeral because Coy
didn't know him and needed help
twelve dollars was almost half what he was getting
he'd never seen her regalia but heard
by reputation how she could make the difference
put her in the choir behind him
even if she didn't know the songs said
Join in whenever you think it's a good time
in full wardrobe including ashes
sat with her head down staring at the floor
so the only thing we could see was the top splotches
where her hair wouldn't grow back in

Reverend Coy did the requisite seven minutes
on the Lord's preacherly love for the church house

to a standing room only crowd when they found out
Lucille Bullard was performing
before he got to Bill Gill and his beloved family
recited scripture where God sayeth
He is the Alpha and the Omega
meaning the beginning and end of time
which meaneth God is time and we worshipeth
our Lord God in this church His House of God
where our beloved brother Bill Gill hath passed
over into the realm of light and time
cradled in the bosom of Aberham where he resteth
in Christ Jesuseth' s folds and Lucille
took that as her cue to raise up from her scrunch
open her mouth where we could see
every tooth that wasn't there
her warshrag soaked eyes puffed up purple
in slits like a Yorkshire sow
sweat soaked ashes pouring down
her face like rivulets of mudwater
or blood if she was wearing a thorncrown
let out a bawl that modulated to a high wail
leaning up toward shriek
her neck quivering like a turkey wattle
or white headed Nebraska yodler
shaking so it might burst asunder as Judas's bowels
every hair left on her head risen to military attention
stood straight out in nine directions
waved that hand with the prominent missing finger
in the air and screeched

there were eight babies in that church house
just as well had been hooked on line
to a circuit board toggle switch
went off at once in a terror scream
all the fire trucks from Lubbock to Floydada would make
at the commencement call for the end of the world
each simultaneously turned and crawled up its mama
immediate verification which ones
had not attended to fingernails

three scratched like cats had climbed their necks
two appeared to be survivors of a rodeo knife fight
in possible need of transfusion
all joining the shriek and wail ceremony viva voce fortissimo
panic beyond the premises initiated by the pandemonium
dogs outside howled at a daylight moon
one screaming as if its foot was smashed by a tractor wheel
birds flew into house windows in flocks
to get away anywhere
children inside bawling under their beds
widows screaming the names of their forgotten husbands
husbands calling for their mothers
wives calling for their lapdogs and house cats
teenagers tossed out of their naps onto green linoleum floors
all the way to Main Street where people came out of shops
to see how many cars involved the wreck
Coy so shocked he reverted screamed
Jesust Christ so loud he was heard above the squalor
then slid back into the adopted method acting character
shouted Has returned among us
people standing up to see if the doors were open
the widow Mizrez Gill told Arty her son Slip up
look in that box and see if they was at the right funeral
him too ascairt to slip up anywhere said No
and he really meant it
then Lucille having achieved the supreme effect
leaned back in her seat in the choir
surveying her masterpiece
grinned like a participant on the winning side
in the first Parliament in Hell

Rufus said later it took every smidgeon
of every calmative lesson he learned
in mortician's school to first get Coy
then the audience and finally those babies
smoothed back down to ceremonial etiquette
didn't even let the Reverend finish his sermon
went straight to the benediction which he
behind the podium into the microphone delivered

nodded for the pallbearers to stand up
come get the coffin right then
closed the lid and wheeled it
through the attendant congregation
on the dolly out the door into the hearse
without even giving the opportunity to file by
and look at Bill Gill one last time
not truly dead but sleeping clasped
in the absolute surety of Christ Jesus's resurrection
turned and told Lucille Bullard
Get up out of that chair and go
out the side door right Now
don't do anything else today

for once in her life she followed
exactly to the red letter edition of the law
what she was asked to do
then when Rufus lifted his hands
like Charlton Heston parting the Red Sea
we stood and marched right up the center aisle
of the house made of time
followed him and Bill Gill in the hearse
all cleansed and perfectly redeemed
in the blood of the lamb
by Lucille Bullard's consummate invocation
of the true essence of catharsis and fear of Coy's God
to Terrace Mound cemetery where Rufus put him to rest
out of the loop and that tragic masterpiece day
dedicated to eternal memory
finally once and for all

STONE WIND WATER

FUGUE
SUNRISE TEA KITCHEN TABLE

> What call'st thou solitude, is not the Earth
> With various living creatures, and the Aire
> Replenisht, and all those at thy command
> To come and play before thee?
> —from the on-line journal of John Maestro Beloved

All night it seemed quiet
until just before dawn

a cricket chir-chirruped
a cicada thrumsisked

a kangaroo mouse scuttled
from the cupboard across the kitchen

its tiny feet thricking on saltillo
the ceiling stretched and crackled

the wall creaked its contrapuntal answer
the saucepan boiled a bobolick bod dob

the water sisished into the mug
the teabag paflumped its belly out

the dog sasdalloped the insides
of his bowl and it claklitit the floor

the mahogany leaves rasheeted the wind
the dry leaves kashie kashied

then a jay cursed and a crow
clacked and khawed and a robin

said *donde* and a hummingbird
phummed its invisible wings by the feeder

and a lost goose awked above the house
a meadowlark tee tee weefee *teewhee teewheed*

the rosefinches and sparrows *djueed teedleeted*
around the grainbowl all their songs

growing wings and flapflapping their way
into a sky stuffed already cramfull with sound

Moonrise Sandstone Waterseep

—after Henri Rousseau

The moon
sprawled across the belly
of a sandstone dune

sky shimmer

Night
fragrant and moist
over
the ossified desert

unpins its dark hair

with a shake and quiet shrug
lets it fall
across the shoulders
the secret archways
of horizon

float into moondrift

Above the dreams
of buried stones
the glitter of a red-spotted toad's tracks
through slickrock
the shining waterseep

darkness closes

stars low on the rimrock
like a crouched cat's eyes
trained on bajada

the joining
the embrace
again

—for Jan, with love

SLOT CANYON

> In the desert there is all and there is nothing.
> God is there and man is not.
> —Balzac

Great smooth stanchions
vault like a slow gesture
across a corner of sleep

The mind's eye rises
to easy invitation
by the memory of sky

Twisted slickrock
tightens inward
gnarled roots tethered in sand

A moonflower huddles
in eternal shadow
against the nave wall

A blue collared lizard blinks
then closes its drowsy eyes
beneath a white blossom

One seamless furl
rock to sand to leaf
to body to white petaled next

As if the desert
turned itself inside out
to contain this moment

Sonatina In the Space

between two mesas
red-winged blackbirds

six in the green palm of juniper
above the graveled floodrace
high-banked

glisten
in the sweat soaked nakedness
of afternoon sun

o-ka-leee

   ***

a cactus wren
chug-chug sings
in the skeleton
of an abandoned pinyon

braided river of bees
work the claret cup

rustle as wind
wanders
the gulch

sweet song of golden light
tumbling
over a mirage dreamed lattice of sea
hanging in the foam
of three quarter day

   ***

a huge orange moon
balanced
on the stretched index finger

of a cholla
rimrocked
on the horizon
poor-will

Autumn Koan

Until the path unspooled its way
between blue granite pillars
and dark pine
to the place where shovels
full of sunlight pour in sluices
scented like ripe pear
the great waterfall
uttered no sound.

Suddenly a trough of thunder,
a sodden roar wrapped in bolts
of blue winding sheet:
the secret drum of the forest's heart
or the drenched kindling stone
of gravity and rushing water
or the sudden and terrifying
voice of God?

—for Eleanor Rand Wilner
homage

WINTER SOLSTICE: MOON NIGHT DESERT

1

Scabland. Sere.
The mesa top pressed flat
by the blue weight of sky,
its gnarled sides
sunsucked crimson.

Yesterday's moon
drowned
in an ocean of canyon,
today's desert sunclotted.

2

Afternoon,
the turbid intimacy
of tattered low hanging clouds,
tangle of cross breeze. Evening,
shreds of late light
snag in the cholla's outstretched arms.

Wind, rock, light and time
form a hinge and fold over
into themselves.

3

The shy sleepiness
of a thin mesquite shadow
in an aging twilight,

bajada
flat on its back,
awake.
The rimrocked moon
astride the cuesta

trembles, rises in a silver shimmer
as a passing of starlight over water
into the dark chamber of night,
curtain, mirror and lamp.

Shadows stretch their black fingers
into the pink barranca,
pull themselves forward.

4

This place of sand and rock
with an ocean's memory.

The desert dreams moon,
feels the tide in her belly,
slow rise of great stones.

The moon dreams sea,
neap and ebb,
dance of wave and ripple
sculptured in slickrock

petrified oyster beds
in the escarpment,
primordial fish
frozen in layers of slate

breath of ocean
in a night breeze
wends homeward
through a rock strewn gully

spindrift redolence
upon the face
in an abandoned stream bed

echo of breaking waves
from sandstone labyrinths.

5

The sojourning wind
tethered to a sprawling juniper

moonflooded desert
opalescent
beneath a bright spill of stars

the creosote's uplifted arms
drenched with light.

—for Ken Brewer 1941-2006

MOMENTS OF DELICATE BALANCE

INCIDENT AT THOMPSON SLOUGH

1

Ollie McDougald said all things considered
which he admitted free and clear he hadn't
next time he'd walk or hitchhike
and if that nephew of his by marriage
on his wife's side ever sat out in his pickup
half of a Monday night listening to the radio
with that one girl in the front seat
running down the batteries
until nothing wouldn't crunk that morning
he'd separate his habits from his ideas
with a two by four or a broke off shovel handle

if he lived to be a hundred and four
he'd never figure out how he let that boy
talk him into getting on a bicycle
with a John Deere teeshirt and a basket on front
to bring the groceries back from the store
on double S & H Greenstamps day
he hadn't rode no bicycle for forty years
but that boy said it's one of those things
you never forget how to do like swimming
or making love to something firm and young
he didn't think to tell him
he never learned how to do moren dog paddle
and he knew for a fact he'd forgot
anything else about the othern
a real long time ago

there he was wobbling down the road
on the way to Piggly Wiggly
boy said he was too tored
to offer to make the towntrip for him
it was only six miles mostly flat
he's sure it'd be okay and the doctor
said he oughta get some exercise anyway

2

It might have been a red letter day he said
except half a mile down the road
here came Coach Bing Bingham from the high school
in his freshwashed car that morning
taking it out to dry and show off said
What's that bicycle you're riding?
Ollie said It's my nephew's by marriage
on my wife's side
he said I can see that it's a red one
where you going to on it?
Ollie said To Piggly Wigglys if I can
make it that far before tonight
Coach Bingham said
Yall want a tow into town?
Ollie said Whar?
Coach said I got a rope in my trunk
we'll tie it to my bumper and on
them handlebars I'll give you a pull
you can coast in the whole live way
Ollie said Not too fast
I aint much of a good
on one of these no more
he said I'll go slow
you hang on and ride
tied the tow line up and got in
then before he started his car
got back out and brought Ollie
this coaching whistle on a loop string
put it around his neck and said
It'll be just fine but if something goes wrong
I don't see it in the carmirror
blown that whistle till I stop
got back in they started off slow
driving in to Piggly Wiggly grocery store
pulling Ollie McDougald on a red bicycle
with his 1957 black brand new production model
Bonneville Pontiac the football boosters presented him
as an incentive to beat Tahoka

shining from the fresh carwash
like diamonds stitched in a bull's butt

3

It was going a squatch better
than Ollie McDougald said he thought
he could have expected
until Clarence Ivie in his pickup
he'd put a new 357 engine in
with cherry bomb mufflers comes
down the road late to get home
in horrible trouble with his wife
because him and his boy
who'd just turned eight years old
at one minute after midnight that morning
in the third grade
named Jerry Don Ivie that fall
were supposed to go up to the store and buy her
Meadowlark butter to make pie crust with
while she finished boiling dewberries
but he heard down to Adolph's cafe on the way
the news that Artie Gill that morning
caught a bass nine pounds and twelve ounces
over to Justiceburg Lake he said
he had to see with his own eyes
before he'd believe it and since
he had his poles in the truckbed
maybe he'd cast out a time or two
let Jerry Don see if it was any
catfish biting on the bottom
which he thought was a real good idea
to celebrate his birthday with

both catching fish
almost a towsack full
two good sized bass and one catfish
Clarence had to help him on
upwards of four pounds
he thought he was pretty sure about

never did see Artie Gill's bass
but they were all talking about it
down to the lake so it must have been
true more or less at least
then he remembered that butter
said Uh oh Jerry Don
we better be getting back home
your mama's going to have her drawers
up her crack if we don't get to the store
went to his pickup
it was a potential tragedy
wouldn't turn over
all the electric flatlined
had to follow it down the wires
until he found a fuse blown dead
piddled through his jockey box
to see if he had anything might work
only thing that fit
was a .22 bullet out of his pistol
he put it in and said Well I'll be
when it worked and the pickup started

pulled out and drove to town
fifty five miles an hour
as an example to Jerry Don of the law of the land
until he came up on Coach Bingham
he'd played football for almost ten years ago
pulling Ollie McDougald on a red bicycle
with a towing rope
came up beside him with the window down
racked his cherry bomb mufflers
hollered Flip a booger on him Jerry Don
just at the same time that boy
pulled one loose and he did
right on the hood of Coach's shiny black car
said I got him Daddy
Coach Bingham hollered Damn you
Clarence Ivie yelled Not if you caint catch me
shifted up to second and peeled rubber
Ollie McDougald said Oh no

4

How could it be but just at that second
Deputy Sheriff Junior Shepherd down
to the four mile bridge cutoff under
the big shade tree taking his turn
showing Maudie Fay Rayburn how the inside
of the new two year old patrolcar looked
heard those cherry bomb mufflers
said By god I bet
that's Clarence Ivie in his pickup
she said Where's he at?
heard those tires squalling said
By god I bet he's racing that pickup
she said Racing it where?
sat up in time to see Clarence go by
on the road like it was Indianapolis
jumped over the seatback
took out the microphone hollering
Sheriff Floyd Sheriff Floyd set up a road block
it's Clarence Ivie coming in to town
past four mile going eighty miles an hour
I'll be in pursuit
said Maudie Fay you have to get out
I'll come back and get you pretty soon
she said Get out where?
Sheriff Floyd called back
on the radio said Come again Junior?
here came Coach Bingham
wide open in his shiny black '57
Pontiac Bonneville honking like a skein of geese
leading in the Second Coming

Sheriff Floyd Sheriff Floyd he hollered
It's Coach Bingham going
wait a minute
Lord God amitey
it's Ollie McDougald on a red bicycle
90 miles a hour blowing a whistle
trying to pass

Get out Maudie Fay
you have to get out NOW
Right here? she said
leaned over the seat and opened the backdoor
pushed her out on the ground
I have to go to work he said Right now
she said You sonofa Bye said Junior
in the office Sheriff Floyd said
Oh Lord I'm afraid Maudie Fay might of
unscrewed Junior's brains out this time
went out to his patrolcar to go see

5

Two miles outside town Coach Bingham
caught up to Clarence Ivie
sat on his bumper
horn wide open
Ollie McDougald blowing his whistle
like a jet airplane and Junior Shepherd
coming off the gravel road on to the pavement
with his red lights and siren screaming
maybe it was the heat inside that pickup cab
or an act of God just then
that .22 bullet went off loud
as a stick of dynamite
tore into the pickup seat up
to the ceiling right through
Clarence Ivie's left testicle
Jerry Don Ivie said he couldn't remember
exactly what it was his daddy said
it all happened quick
and the noise was loud
he remembered the pickup going
into the ditch and him thinking
Daddy, Mama's going to be real mad

6

Clarence Ivie's pickup bounced off the road
into the right hand borrow pit
spun twice and jumped the off side cleft
high centered with the rear wheels
spinning loose gravel forty five feet back
onto the pavement
cherry bomb mufflers backfiring
like 4th of July

Coach Bingham sideslid left axle deep
then sank halfway into Thompson Slough
up to his doors before he could imagine
what happened bellowing like a tornado
said he had to crawl through the window
out on the cartop to see where he was at

Ollie McDougald's red bicycle
turned into a launched skyrocket
over Coach Bingham's Bonneville Pontiac
fifty feet out into muck
before they ceased partnership
that whistle blowing so hard
his face looked like two muskmelons
stuck on his cheeks
bicycle landed upside down in a juniper
front wheel a windmill spinning
like an Olympic champion
Ollie bellyflopped in gumbo
slid twenty more feet up onto tule grass
rolled over thinking he was blind for life
or dead in black hell
until he wiped off the mud
not a single bone broken
or a bloody nose for a souvenir
said he had to pull the whistle up
by the string from where he swallered it
Deputy Sheriff Junior Shepherd
screamed on the scene one minute and

fifty six seconds later
eighty two miles an hour
locked his brakes and skiddered sideways
a quarter mile down the pavement
sank the front end of his patrolcar
into the slough
crawled out the back window and hollered
Yall all under arrest
don't you move any of you
I got reaforcements acoming

Cletis Graves puttered up from his place
with Maudie Fay Rayburn on his tractor fender
picked up on the road if she sworn
she wouldn't tell nobody
Jerry Don lvie screeching
like a banshee when his daddy
pulled down his pants and saw blood
all over his pecker down his legs
said Oh god I'm bleeding to death
holding his privates fainted dead away
Sheriff Red Floyd pulled up
sat in his car looking out at the slough
didn't even recognize Ollie McDougald
so covered up with mud
said the only thing he could think of
was to wonder what the hell
was a bicycle doing with its tires
spinning upside down in a juniper tree
and how come Maudie Fay Rayburn's
wearing Junior Shepherd's policeman's hat
when the radio came on and the dispatcher
Sheila Morris said Sheriff Floyd
it's Darlene Ivie on the line saying
her husband and son aint come home
they posta be bringing her some Meadowlark butter
Junior Shepherd hollering
Yall under arrest
Coach Bingham yelling That little buggar

flipped a booger on my car
Ollie McDougald asking Am I dead?
Sheriff Floyd said Oh Lord Sheila
you better tell Darlene to go get in her car
and start it up
Clarence and her boy been involved
in a incident at Thompson Slough

7

He was posta be getting Meadowlark butter
Darlene Ivie said
Mama said Jerry Don Ivie
Ma'am said Sheriff Floyd
I'd just warshed that car all clean
said Coach Bingham
My car wouldn't crunk and I needed
groceries said Ollie McDougald
Mama said Jerry Don
I caint make no pie crust without
butter said Darlene
Ma'am your husband's in the ambulance
on the way to the hospital said Sheriff Floyd
They was going 90 miles a hour at least
I'll swear to it said Junior Shepherd
Mama said Jerry Don
Did he get my butter? said Darlene
Now look whatall happened said Coach Bingham
They're all under arrest said Junior Shepherd
Here take this you horse's ass said Maudie Fay
gave him back his hat
Mama said Jerry Don
WHAT! Darlene said Jerry Don
Mama Daddy shot off his balls said Jerry Don
Jerry Don I wished you wouldn't talk like that
said Darlene
Ma'am said Sheriff Floyd
Where is my Meadowlark butter? said Darlene
Ollie did you flown that red bicycle up in that tree
upside down like that? said Maudie Fay

8

Junior would you go get this womern
her Meadowlark butter? was what Sheriff Floyd said
that got Darlene Ivie calmed down
and Jerry Don in the car to take him home
so the wench truck could get close enough
to pull Coach Bingham's Bonneville Pontiac
out of the slough and Clarence Ivie's
pickup off the borrow pit ridge
paid Arlis Jamerson five extra dollars
county money to wade out and get
Ollie McDougald's nephew's by marriage
on his wife's side's red
bicycle out of the juniper tree
upside down Ollie said
he wouldn't never ride it no more again
and he didn't want no groceries today after this
double S & H Greenstamps or not
washed his face off best he could
in slough topwater
Cletis Graves went on along after
nothing else was left to see
Junior Shepherd offered Maudie Fay
a ride in to town she said
she'd rather walk
Sheriff Floyd loaded the red bicycle
in the trunk of the patrolcar
Ollie and Maudie Fay Rayburn
in the back seat together
drove them to McDougald's
where they both got out
Maudie Fay said she'd be fine for tonight at least
on the way found out on the radio
Clarence Ivie lost one nut
they'd have to keep him over a couple of days
but wasn't otherwise mutilated
or incapacitated and Deputy Sheriff
Junior Shepherd knocked on the door
when she answered it said
Here's your butter Ma'am

9

Sheriff Floyd Sheila Morris said
from the dispatch office
It's Darlene Ivie on the line
wondering if anybody knows when Clarence
will be coming home and
if anybody thought
to get that towsack of fish
out of her husband's pickup
and bring it by to her house
so she can fix some supper

Big Bend Triptych

1

Cottonwoods

bent over the seep spring
like viejos
wondering what it was

the wind uncovered
and who put it there

a page
from an ancient myth
in need of translation

surely a miracle
to be understood
through the ceremony
of libation

2

Hot

morning sweats with fervor
Droplets
like sin offerings

evaporate into mirage puddles
as believable as salvation
or the serpent's memory
of the garden

Blistered sand
clean as a miraculous portrait
of the Guadalupe virgin
woven by windrift

patiently waits
the monsoon shatter
of pitchfork rain

3

The delicate balance

Santa Elena's shoulders
bunched together
above the quiet river

a dream pathway
for the waxing moon
to carve the letter
of el nombre de dios into sky

above the darkened world
as the river's nubbed teeth
gnaw the slot canyon subway
into granite silt

carrying the great
stone walls
grain by immaculate grain
to sea

CANNONBALL

Hebrews 12:1

1

Yellow Flag

Howard Dale Teaff was
a fast car driver
like his daddy Roy and brothers were
but he misunderestimated his timing
crossed the yellow line his daddy
always said was only cautionary
went out just like them
in a bottle rocket firecracker shower of glory
before he even had the opportunity
to hire on professional like they did
driving bootleg liquor
in from Big Spring
then racing in Lubbock and Hobbs
on Saturday nights

Charles O'Neill lived through
the accident because
they made him sit in the backseat
by himself so the other three
could talk personal that night up front
where he wasn't able
to get flung out and mashed over
Dr. Tubbs said he wasn't hurt or killed any
to speak of in a social manner
but came to the funeral
in a rented wheelchair to make
his memorial pronouncement
so the community wouldn't hold
his survival against him too much
when it was his turn to bear testimony
he said Old Cannonball

was probley my best friend on earth
and right before he went
into the barrowpit and everything
turnt into a blurt mess right up to
almost this ezact moment
the very last thing I remember hearing
him say from his own mouth
as his final words
was to Luther he said Here Junior
hold my beer
I'm gone try something
then the world stood on its head

friends of the family to enhance the service
hired Lucille Bullard
our professional mourner
to come and do a half performance
which was all they felt
they could contribute and afford
at that very moment she commenced
a low moan from the bottom of her throat
that raised hair on all present arms
up to a wattle shaker minor wail
leaning toward potential bawl

unknown to their plans
two high school sophomore girls
who had been known relations
of the non-blood-familial type
to Howard Dale
became simultaneously overfilled with grief
and extraordinary bereavement
from opposite sides of the churchhouse
joined in with matched competitive howls
writhed and bent over hairpulling
so effective not one person
in attendance could have described
any part of the eulogy
Reverend Coy Stribling delivered

his epiphany stolen
right out from under him
us all in a wonderment
at their God's mercy and judgment

2

Checkered Flag

At the graveyard
when the pallbearers placed the casket
on the runner bands
stepped back to take off
their boutonnieres and lay them
on top of Howard Dale Teaff's coffin
the two high school drag race sweethearts
and Lucille Bullard whose salary
for the ceremony did not include
a graveside sorrow rendition performance
together did an impromptu benefit
standing in a perfect isosceles triangle

started with a wail howl
like a band saw
splitting into silver highs
and sheet iron middle range lows
each taking a solo in a perfectly modulated
aria series of coloratura soprano
mezzo and alto dropping to counter tenor
then rejoining and rising
to perfect pitched harmonic crescendo
that could not have been more gloriously
conjoined if Georgie Wilson
director of our world famous
high school choir had color-coordinated
and personally directed it
garnering applause from
a considerable portion of the audience
after which Howard Dale's mama Merlene
seized the cameo moment for her appearance

approached her son's casket
laid an unpaid speeding ticket
among the scatter of white carnation boutonnieres
and said real low but so everybody
there as witnesses could hear
Oh Haard Dell I'm so sorry
your daddy and brothers couldn't be here today
Roy would have been so proud of you
and she patted the end of the coffin
his head wasn't on

walked over and got in her new
used insurance-car and drove
pretty fast some said
back to the Church of God of Prophesy
where bretheren had brought
a pot luck memorial communion
where she went in by herself
first in line
to sit down at the long table
with a black and white plaid plastic tablecloth
in the Sunday School room
and have her some supper
of fried chicken and mustard potato salad
two light bread dinner rolls with butter and jelly
with a side of boiled bacon collard greens
and a large offering of Mrs. T. L. Jones'
first prize blue ribbon county fair
sour cream raisin cobbler for dessert
to conclude the everlasting solemnities
her and her family's race all run

WHEELIS HOUSE: A TEXAS TRAGEDY

> What can these shadowlike generations of man attain
> but build up a dazzling mockery of delight
> that under their touch dissolves again?
> —Sophocles, Oedipus Rex

Dithyrambic Prologue

Fifteen minutes after the trial adjourned
the men's glee club gathered
at the Dew Drop Inn to tell each other
for the first time in a recurrent conversation
how it had been and whatall it meant
Clovis Ledbitter said We might of witnessed
the defining moment in our town's permanent memory
Ollie MacDougald said for his two cent's worth
It could go down as the most important
criminal trial in the history of Texas
but Dan Cockrum who was a printer
and the designated Gateway to the South Plains genius
because Mary Raephelt took her 4th grade classes
on field trips to his shop for forty years
where he demonstrated to a generation and a half
of young Tejas Republicans how he could type
sentences backwards on his printing press
and they would come out exactly right on the paper
which each and every one of us knew was a bona fide miracle
excepting Monroe Newberry who for the first time ever
could actually read it the turned around way
said You two speakers of the house chorus
are destined for immortal greatness because
neither of yall will ever be accused
of misunderestimating the situation at hand
and then he once again created the archetypal epiphany
in the exact center of the proverbial catharsis bullseye when he said
None of any of this might have happened
if Cloyd L. House hadn't shoved his way

into Wheelis's life buying him that damned car
he had to know no boy in his right mind would want
and we all knew he was spot dead accurate
when we put our minds back to that beginning
which set the entire sordid irreversible action in motion
over our copious libations of bootleg Pearl coldbrew

Strophe

Wheelis said By all rights
it should have been the happiest
time of his life but
whatever gods might be watching
over him had other ideas
he'd waited for two years
to get a brand new used car
he could get in and drag Main
chasing women any time he felt like it
but should have known it wasn't going to be
exactly what he anticipated
when his daddy showed him
what he picked out and his first clue
was two toned blue and orange

he even said What the hell
is that? his daddy said
It's a Ford
a good enough learner
Bus Pennel said Hope
you got a good buy on it
his daddy said Yessir
that is a sure enough fact
I bet that will get you son
half a dozen new girlfriends
just waiting to see
what it looks like on the inside
Cephas Bilberry said he didn't think
it was that many blind wormen
in our part of the State
Wheelis's daddy huffed up said

You can take or leave it you don't like it
trade it in on one you want after you get a job
when you got the money to buy one then
took it out for a drive
with his mother and daddy supervising
the commencement of the world
caving in from the top down
didn't get two miles out of town
heard the sirens too late
highway patrol chasing bootleggers
hauling a beerload from Big Spring
over a ridgetop
Wheelis too green to know where to pull off
they plowed into that first new car
on his side of the road head on
like eight sticks of dynamite
mashed his Ford up
into a giant blue and orange plastic brillo pad
killed his mama on the spot
knocked his daddy into a coma
he held on to a week before he died
welded itself around Wheelis
where they had to cut his new used car
apart like a jigsaw puzzle
his clutch leg twisted around on itself
upwards of seven times
one of the firemen said they might
as well take it off with a chainsaw
or a cutting torch
but Dr. Tubbs did it proper in the hospital
bootlegger's car busted apart
slung them into the bushes
one dead and the other one run off
never did figure out who he was
all four doors flung out and trunk lid
blown half way to Tahoka
said it was enough beer on the road
all the fireboys could have
got down like Gideon and had a slurp

only two went ahead and did
all the rest drained in and ruint

Wheelis got a fatwife out of it
when one of the Shoemaker girls
being a nurse for the time being took to him
in the hospital where they got married
him still in bed by Reverend Coy Stribling
until she found out the insurance
was not going to be up to her prior expectations
covered his doctor bills and an artificial leg
that never did fit him where
he could walk on it more than a little ways
without the blister pain on the stub
putting him back on the furniture
until the State finally set him up with a new one
that worked More or less he said
in a hobbling manner
with a used walking cane
he got from Noah Stone's Feed Store
for fifty cents after the FFA livestock show

bills piled up
after his new wife quit her job
found out she couldn't draw unemployment
because she hadn't been fired yet
bank had to foreclose
on his daddy's house he inherited
before she ran off and left
put all his useless belongings in storage
sold the rest over the radio and a yard sale
took all the money with her
left Wheelis laying on a ratty couch
and a foot stool to prop his good leg on
not even a T. V. in a twelve year old used
twenty two foot trailer house
with one bedroom
she bought from her brother on credit
under Wheelis's name

parked under an elm tree
out by the airport no planes ever used
moved to Tahoka and got a job
at the Curl Up and Dye Hair House
running errands and cash register
and the next week
his dog took off and went
down the road toward Two Draw
never saw him again

Antistrophe

then the storage company
auctioned his belongings
because he didn't have
any money to keep up the rent
Charles Huffman said he
seen this barbeque grill
looked like it might have some work
left in it he paid two dollars for
took it home and put it out back
in the yard under a tree
when he opened it in the summer
to see if he could make it cook
about had a brain spasm
it was a laig laying there inside
on top of the grill
like it was waiting to be supper
said after he got through being ascairt
took it in the house
kept it in the closet
except when he needed it to spook the kids at night
to make them stay in their bedroom
until his wife's mother came for dinner
when he put it on a table plate
like it was fixed to eat
she didn't come back any more
after that for a long time
then he got the second best idea
of his life after getting his kids

to sell Grit newspaper and White Rose Salve
and Chapstick tubes for piles
started up a Halloween spookhouse show
in his garage with that leg as the feature attraction
charged a nickel for kids under nine
a dime up to twelve and then fourteen
and a quarter for adults
said people come from all over
the world to see it with a golf ball
painted like Bus Pennel's eye tore out
viennie sausages and spaghettis
with tomater sauce and dog hair
every year spread the rumor
the National Museum in Warshington
loaned him John Dillinger's pecker
in a jar of pickled alcohol
that somebody said he was pretty sure
might be in there
and a womern's privates that was pig livers
and a kidney with some chitlins
in a Mason jar with pickle juice
you had to ask about special
if you were a certified adult
it was something not everybody got to see
one year there was a line half a block long
when Kim Pierce sold tickets
in a dress made for an elf
she slopped out of all four ways
when she bent over to tear them off the roll
and Ella Mae Blodgett stood
behind the leg asking customers
to Please don't touch it
it's fresh and aquivering
and she'd shake to prove it
Wheelis found out about it
went to see the Horrer Show
saw his used first artificial leg laying there
under a farrowing pen spotlight
went straight up to Charles Huffman
said That's my laig you got

Charles said No it's not it's mine
Where'd you get it at? said Wheelis
I bought it at the auction said Charles
I got a Bill of Sale for it to prove it
Wheelis begged him to give it back
for an hour in front of the customers
even said it was a gift to him from his run off wife
and the only memory of her left
it was real precious
Charles said No
Wheelis called in on the radio
and then the newspaper
four letters to the Editor
to take his case to the public
said That leg was his private personal property
that should of never been took away from him
while he was being incapacitated
and reduced to beggary for the rest of his life
any act of decency would give it back to him
Charles said No
it's become a major aspect
of my financial income
I caint let it go
without substantial recompension
it might be worth upwards of one thousand dollars
even more if Hollywood found out about it
and told Vincent Price
he might come and make a picture show out of it

Wheelis got an appointment
went to Judge Parker
told his story from the beginning
bawled in appropriate places to enhance his plea
so much that Judge Parker
called Charles Huffman in to intercede
he brought a valid Bill of Sale
marked $2 Paid in Cash
Judge Parker said Isn't there any way
we can negotiate this?

Charles Huffman said he didn't know
why Wheelis wanted it for
he already had a new one
Wheelis said it was like it was a part of him
that had been tore out of his life
Charles Huffman said he'd think about it
but was inclined to the negative

Epode

finally after two months
of Wheelis coming to the court house
every day sitting outside his office
or in the court room
telling anybody who would
or wouldn't listen about injustice
Judge Parker called them both in to court
for a special trial to resolve the issue
in a private session
so crowded with everybody
who had any way to get there
it was standing room only
to see what might happen

went on for an hour back and forth
with the Bill of Sale even passed around
the court room for proof
then Charles Huffman said
after Wheelis cried in the witness stand
where he swore himself in to tell
the whole honest truth
Out of the goodness of my heart
I am willing to offer Wheelis
joint custerdy of the laig
but he has to agree I get it back
a month in advance to set up my exhibits
in a productive manner
which is by the first of October
Judge Parker said to Wheelis
Would that satisfy you?

Wheelis said What if l wanted it in that month
so I could set me up a Horer House
and make some money out of it?
you wouldn't let me do that I bet
so do I have another choicet?
Charles Huffman and Judge Parker
both said at almost the same time
No

Wheelis House said
I want to dress the court
and after that I won't say no more about it
for the rest of my life ever
Judge Parker said You go right ahead then
we will listen real careful and then we'll be done
Wheelis said It aint no real justice for the little man
like Jesust said If it don't kill you
it will make you stronger
and it's about put me in the graveyard
Irby Metcalf said almost out loud
That wasn't Jesus it was Quannah Parker
the Comanche Chieftain
with blue eyes at the battle of Adobe Walls
my granddaddy was there and heard him say it
This here said Wheelis is the saddest day of my life
I've done lost everything
my car
my diddy
my house
my barbeque grill
my mama
my wife
my dog run off
and now my laig
this is all the injustice
I was ever warned might come
and there's nothing I can do about it
my diddy told me when I was a baby
he was in the war where

he fought and died for his country
so men might have the rights to their privates
and now mine is being took away
where I don't have no control
or opportunity for financial annunciation
using what is rightly mine to get it
but this is the justice I have
and there's nothing I can do
but accept the best offer coming
my wife won't even be here
to testify on my behalf
I'm afraid my dog and my laig
are both gone for good
in a permanent manner of speaking
I have been abandoned of everything
and none of this might of happened
if my diddy hadn't bought
that damn blue and arng Ford
from his brother for bail money
which is a lesson to all of us
life is a line of dominos stacked up
waiting to go down
don't nobody else ever knock that first one over
after that it's all too late and nobody
will ever care or feel one bit sorry for you over it
that's my story

Judge Parker said
That was well done Mr. House
that is your story and I'm sticking to it
I declare joint custody in the matter
of the artificial leg in question
to be granted to Mr. Wheelis House
at any time he wishes to possess it
under the stipulation that it be returned
to Mr. Charles Huffman
no later than the first of October
in order to be set up in his exhibit
in a productive manner

for the entire month of October
is that acceptable to you Mr. Huffman?
Charles said Yessir your Honor
with maybe once in awhile on a Thanksgiving too
when the in-laws might be acoming for dinner
Judge Parker said Is that acceptable
to you Mr. House?
Wheelis scrunched his shoulders
but finally said Well okay then
Judge Parker said That said
this matter is hereby resolved
I declare this case permanently closed
and this court adjourned

Exode

and the men hurried to their cars
to get to the Dew Drop Inn
so they could tell each other
their side version of what happened
which might have been the end
of the story until all Wheelis's teeth
rotted and had to be pulled
and he bought a set of used dentures that never fit
where he couldn't eat ever again anything he liked
we all got to hear about it
when the opportunity presented itself
except he turned around and stared
at the people leaving the court room
bawling like a baby
until almost the last one was left
when he pulled out his handkerchief
blew his nose all into it
and threw it on the floor
said That is a symbol
of my opinion of Justice
and then he and his good artificial leg
hobbled out of the courthouse
with his feed store walking cane
into a bluebonnet sky world
where nobody was awaiting

LAST CALL
AND
DRINKING AND DRIVING

THE MONUMENT TO THE SOUTH PLAINS

Son
your mama who is admittedly a hair trigger weeper
walked all the way down to the barn to tell me
she is genuinely and purely exasperated to tears
with your sitting in here on your bed alone
for three days now wrapped up in divine and superfluous
thought over God knows what and that I
should unleash and afflict upon you a stampede
of accumulated wisdom in order to provide incentive
and momentum for possible confession and redemption
or in other words what in the world is the matter?
your mama really wants to know the cause of your pesteration

Willy John said Nothing's wrong Daddy
I have to make a project in indigenous sculpture
for my Physical Art thesis and I'm trying
to come up with a mental design and materials
with not a lot of luck so far that I can speak of

Behold a wonder said a poet
you were named for once beneath a time son
out behind the very barn where I have been piddling
all morning rests a considerable bevy of red bricks and paving stones
off to the starboard side used cinder blocks and dead concrete forms
on the larboard side a minor subaltern deity's ransom
of worn out farm equipment my daddy put out for years
wondering if there would ever be any use for it
before the Second Coming or the Russian bomb
inside the barn seven sacks of ready-mix concrete
along with arc and acetylene welders and even a soldering iron
I would be just as happy as a crow
that found a dropped plate of communion wafers
if you could utilize that indigenous scrap material
so that it would seem I had a purpose all along
for my years of unrequited salvage, separation and stacking
You got any ideas about what it could be?

Nosir
you go out there and stare at it for a while
if you need lessons on that talent I'm available for instruction
I'll bring along a chair if it takes too long
drawing up a mental plan of opportunity
to endure and prevail as the other man
you were named after once said
build your sculpture any way you want it
as long as it looks good from the kitchen window to your mama
as a monument for the rest of her life
to your teenage years and when you are done
we will call it the Statue of Limitations
until a better title comes along
anytime during construction you think it's gone wrong
give the word I'll knock it down with the tractor
you can start again until you get it right

Willy John built three, tore down the first two
finally settling on a tower amalgamated between an obelisk
and a Babel ziggurat, a spiral of plough shares
fenders and motor covers, tractor seats and steering wheels
a corn planter, spring tooth harrow and flat cultivator
manure spreader, deep trench, disc cultivator and windrower
all manner of painted and rusting equipment
conjoined invisible in the warp and woof, the new body
arose from a blood red brick base
and a gathering of rusty barb wire strung against
an open side like it emerged from the skeleton
of an overlooked and dying chthonic deity
an androgynous Texas god resurrected and ascending from the barnyard
straining against gravity's death clutch
and his father's terrible acrophobia
grasping upward into nothing more than still air
building materials so heavy and bundlesome that at last
Willy John devised and constructed a fifty eight foot derrick
with a block and tackle pulley system to hoick up
a John Deere engine block a magically and technically impossible
six feet above the rig: a great skull atop the megalith
a pair of steel irrigation pipes protruding
like massive horns upward from the sides

after the last arc weld lightning burst
the final acetylene flame, the penultimate binding smear
of cement, wrap of bailing wire, spit and glue
he brought his parents to stand beside the barn
and view the Monument to the South Plains
rising from the abandoned feed lot
and his father trembled, his mother wept
as if she were viewing the birth of a new grandchild
before the great sculpture soughing with the wind's movement
marking the pathway trace of light's footfall
on the near horizon a ripening field of cotton
and behind, knee deep in the white foam of crop
three scattered pump jacks, their rise and fall
like the distant shapes of migrant pickers
working their slow way through the half mirage
My Lord, he said, Willy John, that thing's alive

SUBSTITUTE TEACHER

or

The morning Billy Klogphorne taught the adolescent male Sunday School
class lesson on the designated Christian Leader Preparation
outline topic of Genesis 5: 18, 19 and 23, 24
proving Lamech and polygamy were of the lineage of
Cain and therefore accursed of God
and
Why he was never invited back
to teach Sunday School again

Boys
or should I say young Christian Leaders
potential Deacons of God's true church
I have little to say regarding today's topic
not being familiar with canonized rites of exegesis
therefore this may be a brief experience
in fact the following is potentially the sum of what
I have to say on the matter of Lamech and his wives

Bigamy or polygamy is a crime
That is a fact upon which I will briefly postulate
In a terribly over-populated world it is an inexcusable act
of poor manners, selfishness and stupidity
I do not know if it is a sin
but I cannot imagine or countenance
believing in a Texan god who would condone
much less encourage it
or a Texas woman who would tolerate it
That is my analysis and opinion

Brother Klogphorne
isn't it adultery? and isn't adultery a sin?

Young man
that is a wholly different topic

but in any case I do not believe it is necessarily so
Adultery is recreation
however, it is dangerous contact sport
recreation practiced by all of humanity
normally based upon a lie and because of the lie
it may or not be sin

Brother Klogphorne
isn't lying a sin?

Not always young proselyte
There are categories of both sin and lie
to which all poets and piddlers are exempt
by fact of diplomatic and professional immunity
and all politicians guilty
the divisions being first malicious
and then those designed to prolong one's life, sacrosanct idleness
marriage or commerce with teenage progeny
which should be automatically forgiven
but not so the malicious
which are lies designed to inflate the self like a toad
or tear down another person like a glow worm
deliberately crushed beneath a miscreant's heel
in order to take away or mar what is rightfully his
or in some instances hers

Brother Klogphorne, then what is sin?
the ones they say you can go to Hell for?

Well sir young believer
while Brother Dante Alighieri who well may
have preached a revival service at this edifice some time in the past
did a remarkable job of stratifying hell-bound sin
I will offer the following as my personally updated
Texas-based additional considerations
The only sins you can go to Hell for from any god I could believe in
are murder of one who did not need killing
stealing something of value or precious memory from someone who
needed it, fraud on the part of politicians and currency manipulators

provocations of any war without the intent
of taking an active role in the actual combat effort
that being overt cravenness
and then the ones you're familiar with from this training
designed to produce the next generational crop of deacons
and elders including not being a tithing member
of whoever's church you're talking to
having sex with children
dancing for Baptists and Campbellites
the latter for which it is the Unforgivable Sin
not putting enough money in the collection plate
and malicious and political lying

all others are recreational and forgiveable
or just bad manners
which is why we have wives
to affect and inflict punishment

You don't think adultery
and fornication are sins
then?

I believe I have covered that topic
as well as I am able
the remainder is the parental responsibility
based on familial more and obfuscation
What else can I do for you young potential missionaries?
Mr Klogphorne
can I ask you a personal question?

Of course you may
I am all rimed ears
so you fire away

Did yall have sex
when you were alive back then?

Young man
this being inside a churchhouse

I am bound by oath, covenant, and custom
to tell the truth, the whole truth
and nothing but the truth
so here it is complete and intact
We invented sex

It did not exist prior to our discovery
the world being dystopic and non-functional
My generation gave our youth wholeheartedly
to the definition, methodology and perfection of the practice
up to the point that it exists today
which is the legacy of trust we pass on to you
for final realization and fulfillment

If any of you have doubts whatsoever
as to the veracity of that statement
ask your parents or grandmothers
and I promise you this
Your parents will look you directly in the eye
and lie to you about the subject
as a matter of sacred protection of our mutual trust secrecy
regarding divine inspiration and creation
and your grandmothers will blush and deny that sex exists at all
then go sit somewhere in the cool shade
with a purloined Baby Jesus fan
wondering whatever possessed you to ask such a thing
and that will be your unimpeachable proof
mark my words

Brother Klogphorne
do you remember when you learned about it?

Young fellow sir neophyte
I most certainly do
every one of you in this room should know Maxine Durrant
and if you have not been in her Woman's Store
to buy your mother a birthday present
I am ashamed of, with, by and for you
as she was the most beautiful young creature

in the world since Eve when we were going
about the business of inventing sex
I coveted her as not one of but The pearl of great price
much to my avail as she had little libidinous interest in me
to my great wonder and misfortune
I will divulge this as my incidental role
in the Creation of Sex for the first time in public
She could have read me
the Tale of the Destruction of Sodom and Gomorrah
or the genealogical begettings of the antediluvian patriarchs
and I would have got a hard on

Now as a result of your silence
I assume you have no further questions this morning

Mister Klogphorne
is that where the story my daddy tells
about your stob came from?

Young reverend
I did not know that event had trickled down
like the understanding of federal taxes
to the ears of Garza County Republican youth
I am embarrassed it has come to you
in a potentially contaminated form
therefore I will tell you the entire veracious rendition
of that epic tale complete and unembellished

I was in Maxine Durrant's store purchasing a transparent negligee
for my wife's recurrent twenty-ninth birthday
with expectations of forthcoming exhibition and rejoinder
when Miss Durrant made a comment upon the low riding condition
of my trousers saying I believe verbatim, Billy
one of these days your britches are going to fall down to your knees
I can't imagine what holds them up
whereupon I in Biblical language divinely inspired saith unto her
Maxine, of all people on earth
I would have thought you would know
I have a stob that holds them up
since you are the one who made me aware of it

What happened then
Mister Klogphorne?
Why of course
without further ado she took my money, gift wrapped the package
in a manner harbingering pomp and circumstance
and upon my leaving locked the door, pulled down the shades
and I would fervently wish declared first call
then poured herself a libation before Aphrodite
At least I have faith and hope that is factual
Is there anything else?

Brother Klogphorne
who was Lamech?

Who was Lamech?
Young Master Ivins of the whiplash Epimethian focus
you will need to ask your grandparents
as those legendary citizens from these parts
probably knew him
since he lived over to Justiceburg
as they might say in unspoiled Texanese

Lamech lived at Justiceburg?
Texas?

Young fellers
Acolytes Nutt and Newberry I believe
who do you think wrote the Bible?
Haven't you heard of Eden
and Palestine, Texas? Titus, Trinity and Godley counties?
The Bible was written by, for and about people
not just made up nonsense dictated out of thin air
Of course Lamech Johnston lived out south of Justiceburg
married Rayola Owens and then
Pearl Rae Higgins of the substantial bosoms
after her mama threw her out of the house for stealing
the secret of her daddy's almost perfected perpetual motion machine
and pouring out his bootleg intended home brew,
a moral and conspicious crime which earned for them the reward
of all consequent affliction and reprobation

upon which they moved to the sanctuary of Utah
somewhere west of Eden near a town originally called Hurry Cain
named after his grandfather of preceding generations
who had to rush all the way there to escape
Texas Rangers' vengeance after killing his brother
for stealing a sheep he loved in the custom they knew unto then

you can read about it
in an early edition of the Garza Dispatch
if you follow the scriptures and search out
matters of truth with fear and trembling
in a plain manner of allusionary speaking
But now I see our allotted time is up
so you gentlemen will be needing to depart
and hear words of wisdom
from our beloved pastor the Right Reverend Strayhorn
As my conclusion I fervently hope I have given you young elders
something to ponder over this morning

Brother Klogphorne
we always end our class with a prayer
would you offer it?

Well Lord up there wherever
to say it delicately and in trochaic synesthesia
I certainly hope it was larded odoriferous
with the septical fragrance of churchhouse proselytization
that will linger in these boys' memory for up to nine seconds
then flow down to this community
unadulterated and abridged for time immemorial
and if that is the resultant actuality
I will leave this earth a delighted and thankful man
Amen

Now you boys have yourselves a real nice Sunday
endeavoring to persevere in the effort
not to squirm or squiggle in your pews
but give your devoted attention to matters
of behavioral hegemony and high consequence

***

Did you understand that? said Roy Don Staples
I didn't understand nothing
but that part after Sodom and Gomorrah said Jarvis Griggs
It's Sunday School, you're not posta understand it
yet said Bobby Hudman
I don't think it was pure scriptural said Charles Ivins
How do you know? said Walter Bloodworth
I know it in my heart said Charles Ivins
You don't know Jack Shit said Monroe Newberry
You caint say that in the churchhouse said Roy Don Staples
Nah uh said Monroe Newberry
Yes I do said Charles Ivins

***

Billy Klogphorne strode
from classroom to apse to
aisle to mispronounced foyer
through the church house front door
drove home without an acknowledgment
of sermon or scripture or hymnsinging or prayers
or communion or mandatory collection plate passage
his job as substitute Sunday School mentor and Professor
completed indubitably terse, thorough and Texas true
his lesson to the male youth of Garza County taught
his etched inscription into the permanent memory
of our community established satisfactorily
finally, indelibly, permanently
once and by god for all

amen

IDYLL
THURSDAY NIGHT, ADOLPH'S, LAKE HILLS, TEXAS

This is everywhere I've ever been
—John Sims

Do you like being drunk?

Well hell no
where'd you get such of a stupid idea?
I like getting drunk
being drunk isn't much special
getting over being drunk
makes you wonder
why the hell you did that again
but when you start all over
well that's where the difference is

***

Yall hear about Melvin Ray Bird
falling and busting his ribs?
Yeah heard you found him first
what happened?
He was in his pickup all bent over
like he was ahorseback with kidney stones
I said Do you need help?
he said What does it look like to you?

***

They say now that Odus Millard's dying
he got religion and's making plans
about going to heaven

Being close to death don't mean
you know one goddam thing more
about heaven or hell
than a man who's been married

for fifty years knows about sex
he's trying to remember forward
that never does work worth a damn

***

Melvin Ray Bird's a tough one

Oh yeah he's tough
got two layers of hard bark on him

that's just the part on his hide

***

Was he hurt any?

If he wasn't it'll hold him over
till the good hurt comes around

***

I remember how Odus would set
on his porch furniture awaiting
for whatever might come next
dull as a sop
but alert as a shadebake dog underneath
waiting for any incentive to be abark
any notion come up he could use it as a excuse
for what rurnt his day
I guess I'll miss him anyway

***

What's a matter his leg?
Aint his laig it's his foot

What's a matter his foot then?

He runned over it widge a wagon

A wagon?

What I said

What'd he do that for?

It's a rolling backards he stuckt his foot out
to stop it and it mashed it

Mashed it widge a wagon

Hauling wood

Godamitey

Mash it flat as a duck

Widge a wagon

Full of forewood

Godamitey

Said it hurt all to hell and his daddy
he had to cut his shoe off his foot

Mashed foot

Widge a wagon

How old?

Bout s'em or nine mebbe back then
Godamitey

Why he limp so bad

I imagine

They lose any wood?

Not that I heard of
his daddy was particular but his mama was pissed off
that shoe'd belong to her brother and it was rurnt

I imagine

You'd be right doing that

***

Billy you sure been quiet tonight

I'm trying not to explain to myself
but just understand
how a life that long could have
almost no meaning
beyond the immediate fading of memory
even before absence

You're in it pretty deep I'm guessing
a fire burning in your head

Something like having
the beginning part of a definition
hung up in the cross tangled web of a waking dream
without even finding a word it belongs to

That's a little scary, is it?

then it says Here I am
there I was
and precisely what is it
you're planning to do about it?

That's good enough to be quiet about
I believe so
and I believe I won't be saying
There seemed no man
busier than he was
and yet he seemed busier

than he was
with any reference whatsoever to you
who have been wading with hip boots
tonight I believe

It's a little bit like something
one of us might have done
or thought about doing
just exactly over a dozen times at least

That one I agree with

***

You drunk enough to soliloquize?

I believe so
What's the topic?

Pick one
R. B. you'n Ollie come on over
Billy's feeling loquacious
maybe even Lucretian
or Menippean

What about?

I expect it will be either the Grand Inquisitor
or the lockbox of creation
or something similar pretentious as hell
it's his speech which he'll deliver unpremeditated
and dictated unimplored by his celestial patroness
whilst slumbering he'll decide
Will we be able to understand it?
Nope, not a word

We'll be right over then

I think I'm thinking about that sculpture Willy John made and
how it's wrapped up in time and space. We had to have time

and space so we could have a world and live in it. If we didn't
have time everything would happen all at once and you'd be
your own daddy and son with you smashed and squashed up in
between, which, ironically and poignantly, is exactly the way I
feel at this particular critical juncture of my near-to-end life, as I
constantly feel the press of legacy at my back and my hopes for
the future smashed into my face with the mandatory rejection
of a considerable portion of my own earned and personal
beliefs and ideology by my beloved progeny, all being necessary,
intimidating, and, to a somewhat uncomfortable nature that I
must come to embrace, repulsive in order to maintain a dynamic
world and universe. And if we didn't have space everything
would be a swallowing hole with the sun and the moon and
every damn one of the stars coming right down on top of us,
which, once again, I have come at this juncture to realize is
exactly the way I find myself, trapped in a body that is shrinking,
crushed, and rotting around me while, in spite of the steady
accumulation of evidence to the contrary, I am doing everything
possible to maintain a sense of personal strength and dignity
whilst living within that confinement, continuing to wage war
against the scientific facts of chronology and gravity, fighting the
good fight against my persistent fears of exercise addiction and
anorexia, yet realizing no longer year by year but week by week
at an accelerating pace that ultimately and finally, there is no
fucking way I'm even going to win a battle. That's why they are
the most important. Without them we wouldn't have Newton's
Third Law of Physical Motion. All other things came next, after
that. They 're all waiting to happen or they've already happened
but neither one did until there was a when and a where so
it could, and if there wasn't a that, everything immediately
becomes a wasn't because there would be no documentation.
Thus, it couldn't have been, at least in any objective sense. And
that's how his sculpture works for me, with all his assemblage of
the paraphernalia of the past thrust up into the ether in a manner
worthy of mythological ponderance, what I think it was he was
trying to say and how and why it is. So, gentlemen, there you go.
All of which I've come to understand in the course of an evening
which has perfectly convinced me that I cannot, should not,
and will not ever deserve a claim on any part of that monument

or its significance, which in like manner has brought me to the
realization that for that very reason the one thing I will desire
and lay claim to for the rest of my life is personal aesthetic and
enduring mental ownership of that very object, and I've made
up my mind that I don't have to think about that any more
tonight

What'd you think, Ollie?

I thought it was purdy good
whatall of it I understood
worth a beer I believe
what about you, Clovis?

It was almost a Stay,
thou art so fair moment
glad I asked for it
In the words of the prophet
I believe we heard
something almost being said
I'm drunk enough to almost shed a tear
over that one

Nope, tears are salty
you have high blood pressure and can't tolerate it
besides it's all gravel road
leading to mere oblivion
let's go home

I like it
sayeth all but Jacques
I'm about ready, Billy
let's call it a quit
and get it over with

John Sims' Story: The Oil Well Fire

Lasciate ogne speranza, voi ch'intrate
—Dante Aligheri, Inferno, 111, 9

Don't yall leave yet, come over a minute
and pretend to act like you think
we might actually want you to stay
here, I caint get the top screwt off
this beer I got out of the cold box, Billy
can you or Clovis help?
that's the onliest thing I miss this finger for
I got cut off I just haven't got no grip
to twist off these beer lids
they put them on too tight for me now

they was this guy I heard about
who was a miner or trapper or something
anyways he lived alone up in the hills
I guess mebbe he's a trapper and got it
caught that happens now and then
so he just picked up his finger
stuck it in his pocket and went on home
when he got there he took out his needle and thread
he sewed that finger back on
his hand but it didn't work
two, three weeks later it all swolt up
green and the finger fell off
so's he built a fire in the stove
held the stump agin it
till he burnt all the green poison out
I think a feller'd have to be
pretty much of a man to do that

I knew this other guy loading up
a sow hog and she wouldn't go
he was trying to waller her into the truck
he grabs her by the tail

with one hand, the ear with the othern
she's screaming like hell the whole time
him getting pretty pissed off
he does this a time or two
then grabs her again but
gets the one hand in her mouth
he feels something pinch
pulls back his hand
his finger's gone that damn sow's
bit him off he looked all around
didn't find that finger nowhere
he guessed that sow swallered it

I don't much like to talk about how I lost mine
it still bothers me some
mebbe I'm just too drunk but I started
thinking about it
this all happened before
I went to work for the lectric company
I was younger and hired on for the oil
oh I made good money it wasn't bad work
I don't think I'd do it again
anyways we's up on the panhandle
had a rig drilling about eight miles outa town
we'd work thirty-six on and twelve off
at least I would cause I could make so much
I'd run chain awhile and then crow-nest
never made no different
I was just after the paycheck on Fridays
I'd do about anything they wanted as long
as the money kept coming in and they
seemed to like that
anyways we was down over a mile
damn near seven fousand foot
we knew the oil was right there
we had to be coming through any time
you just get the feeling it's gonna blow
here comes the foman cause we sent for him
cause he has to sez when we can cap off

to get ready for the last push through
so we don't blow all to hell and mebbe catch fire
that foman he's so damn drunk
he caint tell dog puke from crap
starts raising all kind of hell saying
You get this goddam rig running right NOW
we won't hit no sonofabitching oil
for two weeks nobody paid you to think
that's what I'm by god paid for
you just drill till I say stop and then
you just ast how long that's all
now get back to goddam work and stop
trying to set round fucking off

he left and we's so mad we couldn't see straight
for a man to talk to us that way
whether he's drunk or not didn't matter
so we set the bit back down in the night
and let her go what the hell

about midnight the crewboss he says to me
John you go up to the crow-nest we lifting
that pipe out I aint getting blowed up
for nobody and that was fine by me
we's all getting ascairt to where we's just working
not saying nothing just thinking
about how long fore morning or till we got off
it's funny how you think the day'll take
the being ascairt away but it never really does
anyways I climbt up the derrick to the top
we's getting ready to pull that pipe out
all of a sudden the whole thing starts shaking
where I'm about to get slung off
I can hear the crewboss yelling
Get down get DOWN this mama's gonna blow
by god I burnt the palms off my hands
coming down I slid the wire guy rope
to the platform and then jumped off on the ground
the rest of the crew's arredy running ahead

so's I try to catch up and then I hear
that big devil's mother touch off K-BOOM
right behind me and caught on fire
it blew me down on the ground and started
me burning by god I was ascairt
I jumped up and started running and I'd of
burnt to death if this man hadn't grapt me
throwed me down in this ditch and
put the fire out on my clothes

so we look and the whole rig's burning
we can see two guys from the crew laying
between us and the rig burning up
we know they's dead
the rest of us burnt bad where we might die
crewboss he takes off running into the fire
we can see he's gonna try to bring the pickup out
he goes to it and grabs the doorhandle
it's so hot part of his hand
sticks to the door and just comes off
but he gets in and somehow
he gets that damn truck started and drives out
of that fire I won't never know how
all the wires was burnt up
it got so hot that truck's paint was all
scorcht off where you couldn't tell
even what kind of a pickup it was
he brings it to us and we get in
I'm so burnt they had to put me in the back
and I'm laying in this feller's lap
who put out the fire in my clothes
we pull out of there driving like hell
was chasing us to get to town
and by then the fire was so hot
it burnt up the whole goddam rig
there wasn't nothing left and I
seen it bend over just like it was plastic
I wanted to pass out so bad I couldn't stand it
I didn't I just laid there and felt it all
and saw it all

so's we're racing the devil to town
as fast as we can go and we pass this law
he turns on his red light and chases us
till he gets close enough to see and then
he pulls ahead and leads us through town
about ninety miles a hour to the hospital
where he jumps out and runs over and opens
the door and he just puked like hell
three up front was arredy dead two of them
stuck together they's burnt so bad
the crewboss's hand was off
he didn't have no face left
how he drove God knows I don't
there was only one othern still alive and
he died that night so then they come
to get us out of the back and they started to lift
me out I said Get him first he saved my life
the man says it's too late he's done dead
I was laying in his lap

onliest two that made it was me and the crewboss
he was in the hospital for ninety six days
and I was in for a hundred and four
a week and a day more
I remember cause he come to see me
when they let him out
he was burnt so bad I couldn't tell
who he was till he said something
he ast if I's okay and I said Yas
we just looked at each other for a minute
then he walked off
I said Be seeing you, he just waved
three days later he drove his car
into a bridge and killed hisself
they buried him exactly one week after
they let him out and then let me out
the next day after his funeral was over

I don't have no bad scars left that show
my legs is burnt good
I still feel it I get cold
have to wear them long underwears
all year long on my legs
my hands is so thin they bleed easy
skin's about as thick as a cigarette paper
but I'm lucky I guess
all the rest is dead cept me

I went back to work for the oil
the next day because I didn't have nothing
else to do and they put me on chain
wrapping pipes, that's when I done it
I hadn't been working a hour
when this feller on the other side
threw his chain and I felt it hurt
so's I finished and took off my glove
the finger stayed in
I said You sonofabitch you done cut my finger off
I don't think he heard he didn't say nothing
well I had it I went to the man
and said That's it pay me off
oh he tried to get me to stay on
but I lost the taste
didn't care no more

it was after that I went down South
for the lectric company
got my stomach cut out and
then I come here to die
it was a pretty place, I didn't have nothing better
ever day La Verne'd pack me a lunch
I'd draw her a map of where
I'd be if I didn't make it home
I was weak and couldn't hardly stand
so I'd drive up to the caprock edge
where I'd take off my clothes
let the sun shine on me

my muscles wouldn't heal up
on my stomach where I'd been burned
just ugly skin there you could see through
I only weight ninety six pounds
I'd lay on a quilt and look back at the valley
and just wait to be dead and have it done

you know by god I guess I'd still
be laying up there waiting
except after a while La Verne she went
and bought these two hogs for me
she known I'd like that
I got to coming down early to feed them
when I was up there
I'd get to thinking about the market
making money
I got so cited I come down one day early
went to looking for a boar
to get a herd started
the next day I forgot to go up and die
then pretty soon I about quit
thinking about it altogether
it just don't take much to keep
some people going

that gets us about to here
which is nearly last call
before heading home
time for one last beer
they say God takes special care
of children and idiots
I guess he's been watching out
for me and you two
by god I'll always remember them times
they was good times for the most
but I do hope to Christ
they don't never ever come back

Last Call

> The two saddest words in the English language.
> —from a conversation with Bill Kloefkorn

1

Tonight

moonglow
from within
softly

like a candled egg

and softly
stars diminish
until incandescence washes

the dark sky

until midnight's
lightslick
its ebb and flow

liquid

the candent universe
rolls
softly

2

Midnight
remonstrance:

there are those
I wish honestly
only to remember

being gone
and only memory

and
there are those
I wish to never remember

desiring
only their presence

lasting as long
as my life
until forever

as
I cannot imagine
living in a world containing
only their memory

3

And you my friend
whom the gods call
into that other alone

wherever you wake
be it desert or forest
mountain or seaside

find tinder
dry moss and kindling
flint

strike a small fire which
being eternity
will flicker beyond forever

sing
your bright poem
fork your lightning dance

I will find you
sooner than later wherever
you wait in the darkness

We will sing together
delirious and off key
We will tell great lies

to shame the heavens
We will cook with wine
I promise you this

BLUEBONNETS, FIREWHEELS AND
BROWN EYED SUSANS

Slow Waking of Morning from Dream

> The true meaning of eternity is Today
> —Philo

Crows stare
and mutter in foreign tongues
as they line the branches
of a dying live oak,
gargoyles on twilight's ramparts

A white daylight armadillo's tail moon
hangs like a closing parenthesis
south of Polly's Peak
where sun's fingers grasp,
pull the earth down from darkness

Day crawls into bloodshot sky
like an incoming mirage,
spreads a scarlet foam
across the shoulder dunes
of hill county horizon

A sand hill crane hen
perched on one leg
in a wildflower meadow sixty years past—
a feathered memory in dreammist,
head tucked beneath its wing

VEAL, 1948

All afternoon grandmother
dressed the meat
divided the cuts
steaks and chops
a small roast
for the ice box
and sliced the round
into thin pieces which
for the first time
she didn't pound
with a saucer's edge

and for the meal
a private portion
chicken fried
for everyone at the table
including kids
so tender adults weren't required
to do cutting
the savor of fresh beef
filling the air
on the tongue
lingering in the mind

"This is so good"
"So so good, Mama"
"Never so tender"
'Where'd you get this meat?"
and grandmother
head down to her plate
as if in prayer
"Milk cow shed her calf"
"Shed her calf?"
"Still born"

Io sangue voglio, all'ira m'abbandono, in odio tutto l'amor mio fini.
—Cavaleria Rusticana, Pietro Mascagni
(based on the libretto by Giovanni Verga)

Based on an exhaustive, thorough, and complete
Folklore Case Study: Urban Legend Verification
The Authentic, True, and Original Version
Of the Texas Brownie Vengeance[1]

Matador, Texas 1957

Ruby Rushing said her first clue
was a knock on the door
with no post card or even telephone call warning
there stood a perfect stranger
telling two children holding on to her knees
Say hello now darlings
both hollered Hello Great Aint Ruby
ran past her like paired unbroken lapdogs hurrying
to be first to get through the door and into the house
then the woman reached out with a neck hug and air kiss
said It is so nice to see you again Aint Ruby
I hope we're not intruding stopping by
like you told me I should oughter do
anytime I'm in the neighborhood
when I met you at the House family reunion
right after I married LeRoy in 1949
I'm sure you remember me I'm Earlene
LeRoy's mama Mayhewn sends her love
said I could always depend on family hospitality
if I ever needed a place to stay the night
can you tell me where the bathroom's at?

said by the time she could get her situated
one of the kids had her snuff mop and

W. B. Garrett brown bottle in her hands
othern holding up the chair skirt
staring at one of the two spit jars
she had discretely hidden under the furniture
which she salvaged prior to incident
took into the kitchen pantry while they
began opening and slamming drawers
chasing each other through the house viva belezza vocale
asking if she had any toys they could play with
they were already beginning to feel bored

If it's anything we can do to help
with getting supper ready said Earlene
please don't hesitate to ask
sat down in Ruby's personal lounging chair
said It is so much further to Longview
than I remembered I am so proud
you live almost exactly half way back
could I bother you for a glass of ice water
or a CoCola if you happen to have one
how have you been since I seen you last?

said she sat on the furniture and talked
so much Ruby got a new interpretation
of the mystery of the Tower of Babble
while she fixed supper and set the table
got fresh towels and sheets from the chester drawers
made up the trundle for the boy
I hope it's no trouble Earlene said but I'd just as rather
we all three don't sleep in the same bed
Jimmy LeRoy tends to moan and waller
I do hope being in a strange house
don't cause him to have another accident
in the bed he's just a child
we caint hold some things against him
when it's only the fault of nature as we all know
kids pissed and whined about everything she put on the table
I'm not going to eat any of that
What is that stuff there?

This meatloaf tasties like it was raw liver oncet
You don't have to eat it then honey
Mama I don't want no supper can I go play?
of course darling remember not to run in the house
both raced straight to Ruby's bedroom slammed the door

Did you think to make any dessert
for these chirren they both have a sweet tooth?
sat on the dining room chair drinking her cup of fresh coffee
she asked to be fixed for her to settle her stomach
after her hard day of driving
to make it here while her aunt by marriage
cleaned off the table and washed the dishes
then said when Ruby was wiping
and putting them in cupboards
Would you mind much Aint Ruby if I went ahead
and pourn me a hot bath to soak in
so I can be ready to go to bed
after you get this all cleant up?
I'm just getting real tored from all the day's bidness
went and left her shelving leavings in the fridgerator
said it didn't even bother her that much
when she saw the children holding
the glass with her teeth night soaking
whispering about what they looked like
or when they piddled with her radio dial
she couldn't find any of her programs for three days
maybe a little bit or even more than that when they
got into her drawer with her S & H Green Stamp books
which she came in and put in the dishes cupboard
later the soup tureen with the lid on and then
caught Earlene with the door open
looking at the inside like something
might be of interest to her in there
but when she saw them playing with her chapsticks
they'd got out of the drawer in her room
right beside her bed on the table with the Bible
playing with the lids on them
she made them put them back where they got it

then when she swabbed a splotch on her mouth
when she was putting on her nightgown
and knew they'd switched lids
put the white one on the tube for hemorrhoids
brown cap on the lip salve
later heard Earlene talking on her telephone
that night after she'd gone to bed and
Earlene thought she was asleep
telling LeRoy long distance on her number
what them little darlings had done how cute it was
they put their hands over their mouths
and run out the room so she wouldn't know
what trick they'd gone and played on her
Ruby said that was more than enough
for her to have to stand for and put up with
from family she couldn't have picked out of a crowd of two
far as she was concerned it was time
for the Comanches to put on warpaint
stayed awake until all three'd wandered through
her house and the ice box nine times each and gone to bed
for the night snoring and whacking and effluviating
went in to the kitchen and put on her apron
made a big pan of homemade brownies
with marshmallow pieces and dark chocolate syrup
twice sifted Pillsbury enriched flour and an egg
two cups and a half of sugar and a stick of butter
pecans smashed with a rolling pin
between two wash cloths and
folded into the dough and finally
an Eight Day melted bar of Super Strength Ex-Lax cubes
baked and cut into two-inch squares in a wicker basket
with a blue gingham napkin for a liner
waited until after breakfast
where they wanted extra sugar on their frosted flakes
left the soggy bowls all half full on the table
they needed to be in a hurry
didn't even make up their beds because they was sure
Aint Ruby would want to warsh them sheets anyways
the loading up into the car

hugs and air kisses and goodbyes and how
it would take another long day
of driving to get all the way back home
they'd be sure and tell Grandma Mayhewn hello for her
she said Wait a minute
I have a traveling present for you and them little darlings
a small something to satisfy their sweet tooths
went back and fetched the basket
brought and gave it to them through the window
said Wait till your mama says it's okay
before you eat these in the car
and be sure and save at least a piece for her
I hope you'll enjoy them as much
as I surely intend you will Bye now
they drove off and left waving and hollering
who got the first piece

Coda[2]

seventeen minutes and eighteen seconds
after two that afternoon the phone rang
when Ruby answered it
Earlene House said Aint Ruby
is it any flu going round where you live at?
she said Why yes I believe it may be
I could have heard something about that
why would you be asking?
she said I'm thinking these chirren
might be corning down with virus
I just wondered if it could be
something they picked up along the way?
Ruby said That's a certain possibility
some of them flu's spread along nicely
Earlene said I wonder if I oughter stop
and take them in to see a doctor?
Ruby said Oh I doubt it
most of these childhood ailments I suspicion
only last two days or so more or less
then go away natural as it

works itself all out on its own
I wouldn't worry too much just yet
it's only the fault of nature as we all know
the Lord works in mysterious ways
you need to remember
He's always watching out for children and idiots
is our old family saying
you probley ought to get along on home
put them little darlings in their own beds
and you get all relaxed
have you a nice hot bath
from being wore down to a frazzle
after all that hard work
of getting reacquainted with the family in-laws
and driving yalls self all the way back to Longview
if it's any brownies left over
you just have yourself a nice piece
I think you've earned and deserve it
say hello to Mayhewn and bye now
hope yall had a real nice trip to remember

NOTES

1. As told by Ruby House Latham Rushing to her daughters
Annie Sue Latham Wagner, Jessie Rushing Ivy Stailey Brown,
and Ruth Rushing Lee. Repeated to the Research Scholar/Poet-
Librettist by all three sisters on different occasions and retold
by his mother Ruth Rushing Lee after the two older sisters were
deceased.

2. Information in this section corroborated by Ossie and Evert
Smallwood, relatives of Earlene House and in-laws of Ruby
House Latham Rushing, on the occasion of their driving over
one hundred miles to the Lee home for Sunday dinner in 1960
without attending church services that morning after their
in-law Wheelis House had his teeth removed by a dentist in
Turkey, Texas, he accompanying them and complaining, "Ruth,
it isn't anything on this table I can eat," whereupon the Research

Scholar/Poet-Librettist's mother passed him the gravy boat, but with a different interpretation of tone; from their point of view, the story, while true in factual data, was a betrayal of hospitality and an act of deliberate severance of ties established by marriage, leading to disinheritance, disavowal, and schism wherein she (Ruby House Latham Rushing), in their own words, "declared unpervoked war on her own family and in the eyes of the whole neighborhood turned the reputation of the House family into a pile of shit."

For my son
upon completion of all requirements
for his PhD in Folklore

Matthew 3:17

February 2009

ETYMOLOGY/DICTION
OR
THE EARTHLY BEATIFICATION OF MISS LILLY MCCREE

>She's the Lily of the Valley
>Our bright and shining star
>   —variation on a recalled hymn from my childhood

Lilly McCree rode herd
three generations on our town library
according to Ollie McDougald
taught every kid she met
what Mr. Twain said
He who will not read good books
has no advantage over he who reads no books
so even Goose Landrum
who was the embodiment of the second he
knew that maxim by heart
and gum chewing, whispering
or talking in the library was an abomination
answering to God Amitey at the Last Judgment

she became famous the first time
when Jiggs King got the Dispatch
to publish articles his Occupations Class kids
wrote as Spotlights on Workers in Our Community
sent Howard Lee Taft to do an interview
with Miss Lilly at the Library
then didn't bother to read over his essay
before it got submitted and published intact

Howard Lee started by asking
Was being a Liberian your first job you ever had?
she said Oh no
my first employment was as a waitress
at the Last Supper
he said Oh I didn't know that before
asked her to Go slow so he could

get it all wrote down in her own words
she made sure he did just that
so the whole town learned Bartholomew
he spelled Barnapple
paid the bill and Peter was Scotch
believed in only tithing
left the tip, a widow's might
and No she wouldn't truly recommend
waitressing as a Lifetime Occupation Choice
but she enjoyed liberianing
as it gave her the opportunity
to share her true love with both women
and men of all ages
who could read about it
as well as do it in person with each other
at the liberry or in the privacy of their homes
if they checked it out first

but the crowning pinnacle star in her halo
was bequeathed by our community
that day she stood face to chest
with Larry Joe Williams outside
the Church of Christ after services and handshaking
looked right up into his eyes
and clarified a principle
of temperament, language acquisition and usage
the entire near-monologue witnessed,
overheard and perfectly imprinted
on the memory synapses of three teenage boys
who interrupted their post-sermonic
philosophical discussion on the interpenetration
of truth, goodness, sex and football when Miss Lilly
opened her mind and heart that day

Larry Joe was neither loved,
liked, cared for, respected or preacherly tolerated
by anyone in our town
nevertheless a legend in his own mind
and his personal choice to be

Town Councilor, Mayor, Judge,
Justice of the Peace and Church Deacon
in the soonest possible order
as prelude to State Governorship
then perhaps a run for the Holy Grail
unseconded by anyone save his wife Laura
who spoke in such a still small voice
his self-nomination always declared itself
dead for lack of any known support
still he campaigned lustily and desirously
throughout the city from church pew
to Ingram's Barber Shop to the aisles
of Piggly Wiggly to Elder's Council
but hamartia's arrow flew into focus
when he attempted to address the issue
of his being passed over for Campbellite Deacon
inside the vestibule of the Public Library viva voce
only to be forcibly ejected out the front door
by Miss Lilly, a woman less than half his size
yet his equal in conviction and fortitude

still he persisted, even invoking Titus 1 dot 6
to remind the Elders' Council that T. C. Clark
had only one believing child
while he and his lovely wife
in the first four years of their marriage alone
brought forth four future proselytes
as the ocular fruit of his loins
not mentioning the fact of the first child's birth
occurring six months and seventeen days
after their wedding took place
or that his wife Laura presently carried
a fifth child as a result
of a prolonged evening of libations
in a futile attempt to procure acceptance and membership
in the Men's Glee Club at the Dew Drop Inn
items much discussed at the regular
monthly Eastern Star meetings
then taking the pulpit just before

closing prayer that memorable Sunday morn
to address the congregation regarding
the matter of his being passed over
once again in spite of his family's best efforts
he begged immediate intercedence
by his Christian brethren and sisters
in the matter of this unrighteous injustice
after which he walked up the center aisle
reserved for the preacher prior to benediction
to stand outside over by the pavement
and await their truly righteous sympathetic
condolences and outpouring support
to get this all turned around and made holy and correct
before God and the Public at Large

the only acknowledger
of his presence was Miss Lilly
who walked straight to his corpus
and first stared a direct line ahead
into the middle of his sternum
then lifted her face until she
peered straight up into his squinty Poland China eyes
said Larry Joe
while I may eventually be self-chagrined
for interrupting the exuberance
of your desire to be noticed
I want to offer you my sincere and humble thanks
emanating from every fiber of my being
and he said You want to thank me?
Miss Lilly said Wholeheartedly
Larry Joe said Well fine but how come?
she said All my life
I have engaged in a love affair
with the written and spoken word
devoted myself as Custodian of Culture
to honor the right literary, civil and genial
use of language which I have always
considered deity incarnate
until my contact with you

I believed we had sufficient wordage
such as malarkist, buncombe, vacuous troglodyte,
lambent dullard, cornaptious miscreant
all perfectly acceptable terms short of verbiage
for the socially and intellectually execrable
therefore I had never comprehended
manifest need for the coinage and usage
of the nominative cocksucker
prefaced by the adjectival stupid
to create what seems on certain occasions
the formation of a perfect inferior syllogism
until now
and thanks to you
I shall never again be confused
by that etymological necessity
for the immaculate riff-raffian appellation
for that I will remain in your debt
for a period of time extending into eternity

and then without waiting to hear
Larry Joe Williams say Huh?
Miss Lilly like neon Moses coming down
the mountain carrying the law in his pocket
walked to her 1948 Studebaker
in the Church of Christ parking lot
and drove home to *looke adoun ... and think on Christ's passioun.*
and eat her Sunday dinner, all alone, beatific

POSTMORTEM: AFTER THE OBSEQUIES

1

What I remember of the past first
is a day during those days
when I wanted to sing opera,
a day when everything happened
that I cared to be inside the happening thereof:
rain crushed through the live oaks
in a wild sprint, then circled
into the meadow like a band of Comanche warriors
flashing bows and spears, come in bright warpaint
to carry me away to join Cynthia Ann Parker,
the sky filled with attack screams
and distant drum roar,
just as quickly the meadow empty
and quiet, storm moving
away like a stampeded remuda,
the world all bright color
and me right in the middle
living my life inside a rainbow

Then a three quarter waxing moon, half risen,
wallowed in the tank with a modicum of enthusiasm
and emphasis, like the teenage girl I was,
alone, shy, and waiting for no one
under the fall of perpetual nightjars
Lords of the Dance
carving traces in the sky
with their joyous roar in the feathered twilight
and into that memory traipsed
Charles E. Carr, Jr. the Second, who was my first
and only suitor to whom
I was conquest and chattel,
the fact of which I was reminded
weekly and at times daily,
not to mention his boast

thrown to anyone who cared to listen
that he won me in a Gin Rummage game,
a man who had the commanding presence
to fill any room he entered
like the effluvial waft
of digested butter beans
telling me, "Bull bats, Merlean,
insignificant night birds
that never even learnt to sing,
that's what this is all about. Bull bats.
Seen one, seen 'em all."
And, with the end of magic in my life,
I became his wife.

2

It wasn't all that long after the wedding almost nobody came to
when I remember the air that one morning, still, like it was hold-
ing down something dying to let it finish its work, and if I made
any movement, even turning my eyes just a little to see if any-
thing around me was alive or even breathing, I could feel little
pocketswells of cold like current spots swimming in a lake sky-
bolted above the earth, but standing perfectly still I was in a hole
in the universe with nothing moving, only the suspicion of death
walking an invisible circle around me, then the hardest thunders-
mash I've ever known lifted and pitched me against the ground. I
couldn't breathe but still I tasted what seemed the color of green
and my blouse stuck to my flesh like my grandmother's jalapeno
jelly, melted chili pepper rivulets down my back and I remember
thinking that's where my wing sockets could have been and now
they're cauterized. My hair tingled like I'd just shampooed with
yucca root and wild mint and it stood up with gooseflesh shivers
that washed over me as if I'd fallen into a deepwater well. When
I looked up, all the laundry on the clothesline had little halos
on them and I laughed out loud, glad Charles hadn't put any of
his underwear in the basket that week because he would have
seen it as a personal miracle. That was when I heard the music,
the whole sky singing and throbbing and all the trees with all
the bright colors I could ever imagine dancing their sparkling
leaves to the rhythm and I knew somehow right then before I

had any time to think about it I was the only one who could hear it. And there he was standing right beside me and the first words he said were, "Where you been, Merlean? I was walking all over and couldn't find where you was at. Didn't you hear that lightning? You shouldn't be laying on the ground like that when it's looking like storm, you could get struck dead and rained on. You better get on up now and come in the house and think about fixing some dinner." And I saw a daylight moon right above me pulling apart the thickets of clouds so it could look down and see something it was hunting for, almost like it was searching out the earth's tide pull-trigger and I knew I was re-alive and that I'd walked through the doors of a crypt nestled in the back of an ancient cemetery from once before a time. And the breath of musty air wrapped me up in the fragrance of a salvation I'd never dreamed of, like everything I knew and believed up to then was bound up in the rusty leather smell of a closed book on a Sunday morning that never was and I was a child again with all the world before me, and I knew there was nobody in my life I could ever tell it to until this day. And I got up and followed Charles into the house. Fifty four years ago.

3

In the spring of '54
I bottled fourteen quarts
of tornado

every time he made to leave home
he would find them
in the back of my closet
and open one

the house looked
like two three year olds
and a teething puppy went through
this one time looking
for his reading glasses

behind Piggly Wiggly's
he found a copy of last week's

TV Guide
wanted to see what he'd missed

I guess I made them
for his libations
the missing excitement

since he said, "It aint
no color in my life."

4

I waited outside on the sidewalk that day
he went in to Bob Collier drugstore
ordered himself a limeaid
with Roy Rogers grenadine syrup
and a straw

concentrating so on his drink he walked
into a street post a half block down
spilled Roy Rogers all over his front
stood on the sidewalk and yelled,
"Well God damn Merlean."

The closest store was Maxine Durrant's
I went straight in to the panties counter
when I looked back he was standing
staring with his ruined shirt and empty soda cup
through the glass door

I picked up a pair of bright red ones, French lace,
shook them out, held them up
turned toward the door with them over my face
counted ten, lowered
he was gone

Maxine said,
"What are you doing, Mary Lynn?"
I told, she giggled like Alisoun in "The Miller's Tale"
so long she locked the door

pulled down the shade
she went to the back
brought out each of us
a paper cup of good time
she said, "It's an occasion
for us to have a girl party."

5

He went all over town haranguing, wrangling
and bargaining like the Scotchman he was
when Charlie sent him that birthday check
because anything he bought for him
would somehow be taken as a personal offense
and had to sign the card Charles E. Carr, Junior II
so he wouldn't feel the slight to his patriarchy
that money burning a hole in his pocket
he conned Gordon Hamilton down to sixty-five cents
under Bill Edwards Hardware for a silly electric razor
never even knew Gordon Hamilton called me
to bring in the sixty-five cents from my personal egg money
being perhaps the only chincier man in town

so proud of his brand new Braun electric razor
he'd made such a good financial deal for
and then like some Texas deus ex machina
whatever god looking down with a sardonic sense of humor
that day smote him with a case of shingles
there wasn't anything Dr. Tubbs could do
a thing about except prescribe calamine lotion
and tell him he was forbidden to shave
until the disease had run its course

forty days and forty nights Charles E. Carr Junior the Second
sat in his chair and watched the television set
rooster crow to midnight shut down I learned to pray
to come quickly like Christ's Second Coming
until I knew every program on either one
of the two channels we got from Lubbock
he didn't even have to call from the barcalounger

when it was time for me to come in
and change from seven to eleven or vice versa
it was as ingrained in my memory as catechism
or my time of the month, the whole world
inside that house turned to black and white
Howdy Doody to Lucille Ball to Friday Night Fights
which I would have loved to sign him up for
against any world champion mean and available

I remember the day when I received the revelation
and understood the true meaning of the Biblical flood
how that story had not one thing to do
with the man named Noah but with his wife
who had to endure forty days and forty nights
locked up in that boat with him and all those animals
being at twenty-four seven beck and call
barn swamper, feeder and nurse mom-maid
mother-in-attendance, cook and bottle washer
with nothing more to look forward to than
getting off that damn ark after it quit raining
and start being pregnant again so that
he could fulfill his duty to replenish the earth
thank god the good Lord had changed
his mind about the subduing it part
that would have been one too many for her
and the other thing of it is, we never even
got to learn what her actual name was
I doubt Noah ever mastered the pronunciation

the whole time he sat in his chair
with that razor in his lap like it was
the Ark of the Covenant to see him through the desert
of his personal affliction and could I please
bring him another sody pop or a sandwich
or run down to Piggly Wiggly and get him some
chocolate chip cookies he had a sudden craving for?
only interrupting his meditation on injustice
and the television set to hold that razor
up to his ear and turn it on so he could listen

to another source in the world capable
of producing an immaculate meaningless whine

6

Philippians 1:21

And he said, "Bretheren,
Now is the time of mourning,
The time for weeping of tears,
But this, too, shall pass and go away
As we learn the Plan of the Lord's Great Will revealed
That yea, it cometh to pass each and every one of us will one day
Die and pass and go away and be dead and gone ..."

and I thought Holy God
Jesus Christ and the Catholic's
Holy Mary Mother of God
if that's the best he can do
the Apostle Paul hater of women notwithstanding
I could be preacher
at this church

7

Coda: Last Call

*In the darkest cleft of midnight
a tiny wisp of silence cowered, concealed,
hidden by a cowl of wind*

So
grief, like love,
is work
that has to be done
and
I have no clue
how or whether
to begin

I read once
I don't know when or where
or why I remember
that Rossini
said he only felt grief
twice in his life:
when his mother died
and when he was on a boat
and a roasted chicken
stuffed with truffles
fell into the water
lost and gone

I know I grieved when mama died
again when Honey my best friend dog died
once more when Charles, Jr. left
for school and I knew
he would never ever really be
my little boy again
but before God I do not know
if what I feel is grief
or something else
I don't understand
can't name

I've never known the taste of truffles
but I've lived a life
cramful of trifles
          like
a bowl brimful to sopping over
with a concoction whose magic ingredients
I can't remember
slipped out of my hands into the sink
a potsherd broken away, everything spilt
and I don't know which to mourn
the lost recipe
or the bowl
and because I just don't
feel like bawling or cursing

or starting over another supper
I can only stand and stare
at the suption draining away
into a whirl
Lord God
it's one of those alone
hard red wine nights
foreshadowing a bloodshot tomorrow morning sky
spiral broken moon splinters scattered
all over the floor and on the furniture, lying
like breathing, open-eyed antimacassars
daring me to come sit anywhere near
pushing me out the back door scared
into the big alone

Oh, but breathe in the waft of a ghost rain
under a waxing cat scratch moon
floating through live oak
listen to the memory of a waif cinder maid
singing Una Volta C'era Un Re
and beneath me
exactly between my feet
a perfect moon-scarleted primrose
glistening in the rekindling of the night

Nocturne Idyll
Ike's Grocery Store, 1962
Saturday, 9:55 p.m.

Suetta Rushing met Laveda Latham
coming out the door
said Oh I'm glad I made it in time
I have to get something for dinner
for after church
did you forget too?
Laveda said no
she only needed mushroom soup
Oh yes said Suetta
that's real good
to put over leftovers
so they'll look freshmade
And green jello said Laveda
but so she wouldn't be rude
asked Suetta what she was having
I'm getting a whole half a chicken
to put in the oven
with Arsh potatoes if they
got any left she said
and mayonnaise and walnuts
so I can make a Waldorf salad
like they do at Hemphill-Wells
for their luncheons in Lubbick
I better get in before they close
the doors and plumb shut me out

Oh said Laveda
they wouldn't leave you outside
that's what they're here for this late
Well that's just exactly right
and there's no use to talking about it
and idn't that sweet of them said Suetta
they're such nice neighbors
and idn't it fine to not

have to get dressed up
to come to the store like
it was Piggly Wiggly and
idn't it a right purdy night
is all I have to say
about that subject

and they looked up
as if it was the first time
to a sky where Scorpio
held Saturn in its claw
like a jewel
dug out of the bedrock aglister
beside the ripened Cheshire cat sliver moon
the whole world awash
in wind crushed cut hay perfume
roar of cricket song
pouring down our town's streets
up the caprock, across the high plains
out over the hill country
the night beautiful and mysterious
as an old friend's ghost
moving toward shadow, waving back
from an uncovered memory

MINE TAILINGS

SILVER CITY DAWN PSALM

This time right here, Lord,
in this room of light and shadow
where kindled winds breathe
the world crackling awake
with sage redolence

rise of quail scuttle
and Fred's rattlesnake-killing cat
wading autumn's leaf garden
homeward through the arch
of sprawled golden branches

> *pinyon fire & coffeeboil*
> *gurgle-steam the bank*
> *of Comstock kitchen walls*

the tired old sun stretches his long arms
pulls down eastern horizon
with a yawn and sigh
one more time shoulders his pack
and begins the high lonesome saunter
　　　　over Sierra

for Fred and Las Swanson

MONOLOGUE: SOFT FOCUS MEMORY:
OF GETTING DRUNK WITH A SCIENTIST
WHO ACTUALLY READS

Here are the data:

the half life
of a butter bean fart
is eleven hundred years
Now
if or when that figure
is bumped
by the factor of two Lone Star beers
the half life is not altered
but the velocity of impact
is increased by pi
to the tenth power

but I fear, amigo colleague of mine,
trying to impose advanced pedagogy
at this hour
is akin to catching piss in a basket
or moonlight with a fishnet

Nevertheless
I am ravished with admiration
for tonight's libation and discourse
while humiliated by the impossibility
of holding that same piss in
all night or attempting
to sleep in a hurried squatch
as I have a nine o'clock tomorrow
which will require an exuberant lecture
one of my self-reproducing
cyclical and incestual peccadillos
to stimulate young minds
to the Olympian heights of splendipity
in full knowledge

that I have been
a bell with a loose clapper
pealing at the incessant rate
of 768 miles per hour
or in a confined area
4.689 miles per second
a grandfather clock stuck
on the perpetual monotony of twelve
a sot howling like a troglodyte
at the full moon

ergo now you must
push me out the door
and point me toward home
I will fall in that direction
at the speed of 32 feet per second squared
or prepare thyself
for permanent adoption
to the footsteps of infinity
of a pound dog genetic mongrel
of unidentifiable DNA

Good night sweet prince
and angels waft thee
as I make my way into dark matter
and the extreme possibility of black hole

Please call my lovely wife
tell her not to pay the ransom
I have escaped
and am in the tesseracting modum
turn on the goddam porchlight
which will broadcast its presence
at the velocity of 186,000 miles per second
I am coming, Dear!
Lead me gently home, Father
Prepare for re-entry and touchdown

RAIN AUBADE: AN ARS VIGNETTIA OF SORTS
BOULDER, UTAH, OCTOBER 2018

> Time hath, my lord, a wallet at his back
> Wherein he puts alms for oblivion
> —Shakespeare, Troilus and Cressida

A taciturn and sodden day when the words traipse and stand apart in galoshes, agape, muttering unwillingness to join and distaste in all concepts for belongment, refusing allegiance to stanza or paragraph; when intermittent clusters form, no conjoining or gathering, a seeming falling away from any broken trail where language can rise, separating from the body to the lift of delight, today only the insolent downward tumbling toward the imagined desert labyrinth of evaporation, desiccation.

Mudstuck and estranged between image and word he removed his glasses, closed his eyes, and lifted an open hand, begging alms. After a small eternity, in the reimagined world a hummingbird hovered an inch above his palm, a shimmering rainbow, the miracle between storm and light.

for Diane Oberhansly

AUBADE

A Love Poem
9 November 2016

Jan transfixed in dawnflay after the longest night of her life in the swollen
eyed kitchen, lost between thought and next somewhere spanning
mesmerization and death meditation. Beyond the window a figure,
hunched into the cold and shuffling, made its way uphill toward our dome
on the rock. Somebody's coming, and Jax barked, and Jan said What?
Look and she looked through the barest orange wisp of an insipid
harbinger of sunrise and said Hush Jax, it's Carol and she went to the door
and out and our birdfeeding neighbor with the yard of glorious flowers of
all colors, now gone with the season, opened her black coat in the gravel
driveway to a bottle of white wine and both women stood bleary and
looked at each other and then fell into embrace with Jax just aside
looking up at them in wonderment beneath a daylight almost translucent
half moon above the sleeping woman horizon, lost and frail in the empty
Sierra sky as the ghost of an almost forgotten terror, they clutched one
another and wept and wept.

INCIDENT BASED ON A TRUE STORY
SEEN ON CHANNEL 7 LUBBOCK EVENING NEWS
SOMETIME PROBABLY IN THE 1950S

> Artists are here to disturb the peace.
> —James Baldwin

1

Harold Wheatley like Judas
thought he would go for a walk in his garden
being 80 acres of purdy good looking
August cotton on his birthday that morning
when he was struck on the very top metal button
of his Intermountain Farmers ball cap
cumpleanos gift from Ramon Martinez
who got it at a thrift store in Paragonah, Utah
by an ice ball falling out of the sky

Did it kill him any? sed Ollie McDougald
down at the Cotton Mill loading docks
Bobby Reid sed Killed him severely two days now
George Tillman sed he heard it was
a giant bluesky hail stone, a miracle
hail ball made out of shit
sed Cephas Bilberry when it got through melting
I'll swan sed R. B. McCravey is that gospel truth?
That's what they say pure shit sed Cephas
pieces of corn in it you could still see
Busted his head open like a two penny party balloon
is what Dr. Tubbs sed in his own words
after the examination sed Travis Stribling
whose wife was being the fatnurse at the hospital

We all agreed Rufus would have
a real hard time getting him reassembled
so there could be an open coffin funeral
we'd all have to get dressed up
and go see for ourselves

pictures being untasteful
therefore unlikely forthcoming
Harold would have done the same thing
in our place

2

Every airline from Lubbock to Dallas
to Albuquerque denied any flight
over the South Plains that morning
there was not at all no way
none of them could have had nothing
to do with it they were pure innocent
they would swear an oath to it
it must have been something picked up
by a careless tornado swooped
and held in the sky until it froze
then fell of its own violation and gravity
just bad luck he should of
stayed in bed that day
an act of God merciful in the suddenness

3

After the funeral the widow Mahoda sed
she was the unluckiest woman to ever live
and she didn't want to talk about it, but
now they would put it on the television
and then in the newspapers all over
with her picture of the grieving
all the rest of her life mired like a sow stuck sideways
in soured hogmud with the memory of being the wife
of the farmer killed by a thirteen pound turd
flushed out from a damn flying saucer
wandered off course and lost over the Llano Estacado
one hundred and eighty seven miles from the Roswell landing strip
undoubtedly accompanied by canned laugh track when Jimmy Issacs
the announcer sed her name
out loud on the six o'clock news showing her face
on the TV, not a thing she could do

but live with it, not one iota
to ever be thankful for the rest of her life
insurance barely even paid
for the funeral, goddammit
it was all just an embarrassment
a dammed crying shame

Silver City, Nevada
Thanksgiving Day, 2016

WHAT MY GRANDMOTHER TOLD ME
WHEN I WAS FOUR
AND WE WERE MAKING SOAP

You have to boil the lye
in a large kettle over open fire
till the scum floats to the top

then you pourn it off
onto the ground and let it kill the weeds
and keep the clean for soap

the separation of lye and scum
being the first stage in the creation
of personal hygiene, decency and cleanliness

the key principle being
bring things involving lye to a hot boil
the scum will always float up

GLOBE MALLOW REDUX:
HOUSEROCK VALLEY

Turn out right there Jan said
and I said okay and
pulled off the highway
and Jan got out with her camera
started taking pictures
Globe Mallow spread thigh high
across the red desert
thick as Moses' sea
tangled with Pharaoh's chariots

then another car pulled off
and another then one more
all of us like children
in a field of strawberries
stretching to the edge of horizon
lapping over into otherworld

and then the '84 Ford
with Louisiana license plates
doors flung open
driver bolting for a ditch
and a long bleeding of the lizard
passenger sauntering toward us
eyes agape, neck turning
Whatchyall looking for
is it some dead bodies out heah?

Jan gestured toward the wild flowers
turned back to pleasure
he turned to me
What all yall taking them pictures of?
I said Globe Mallow
we've never seen such profusion
Seen such of a what?
The flowers I said

What'd you say they was?
Globe Mallow
Like marsh mellers? he said
and I said Exactly
they are in bloom like we've
never seen before
That where marsh mellers come from?
and I, too, thought hard for us all,
My only swerving
and said Yes
they're in full bloom
and this fall they will have fruit
spread across this field
like high caprock Texas cotton on a rain year

Is it worth any much? he said
And I said Yes, so I've heard
a four ounce bag in a grocery store
goes for two dollars I've been told
and a tow sack full might hold
what? one hundred pounds? at four
two dollar sacks to the pound
and he said Jesust Christ

can you pick it?
and I said On the outside
of the fence, inside is Reservation
only the Navajo can harvest there
that's how they get all those new pickups
this side of the fence is BLM
and belongs to the American public
You wouldn't be shitting me now?
and I said No sir
I am a retired Professor of English
and I have neither patience
nor respect for hyperbolic felicity
that being beneath my dignity

he said You swear to God?
and I said Yessir
I will swear to whatever god you believe in
that that's exactly what I said
Jan was staring at me with her look
I shrugged in the sunlight
hoping I was bursting into blossom
Looks like it's going to be
one hell of a crop this year
but he had already turned
striding toward his car
with purpose and enthusiasm
LeRoy he yelled Whar you at?
Get back to the car
I got me something to tell you
hurry up goddammit

a rip-snorter for Bill and Dorothy
Te amo

Dream of Adoration

She said Last night I had a dream
and the voice in the dream asked me
what it was I wanted most of all
I said Most of all I want
to some day be adored that is what,
and he said That is real simular crazy
because just some while back ago
I had this dream about could I
be something besides me
and what would it be and the voice
said You wanta be a door?
and I thought that might be something
I could be good at, the way in and out
of wherever anybody wanted to be or go—
I could maybe make a difference that way
and then I saw them putting me together
out of green wood with a rip saw
the edges uneven with no T square—
only two brace beams where I'd fit all aloose
with used hinges so I couldn't
never be 90 degrees and punk wood lockstobs
with oversize holes so they dangled like pigtails
on both sides where the door wobblied and not
stayed shut tight on either side in or out sigoggling
and they put me on a outhouse off to one side
where I beat and banged and flopped
and squawkcreaked and flung open with
the slightest wind at the always wrong time
and then there was daddy bellering
Goddammit boy what the hell good are you for
you don't even make a decent shithouse door
how in the name of God did I ever get a boy like you?
and then I seen them come to get me
took me off down behind the barn
where I waited in the weather alone
until here they come with axes
to chop me up for forewood

and that's when I woke up and known:
I didn't want to be no dammed door
or anything else, it was then I give up
on aspirations and decided I'd have
to be whatever it is that I was
set out to be and just learn to live with it
right up to the end unless I chose sooner
And neither one of them said anything else
just sat in the car at the Sunset Drive In Theatre
watching Gregory Peck and Audrey Hepburn
that one day they had alone together
and ate popcorn out of each other's sacks
until the picture show was over
when he drove her back to her house
all their adoring dreams permanently deferred

AUTUMN ECLIPSE
SEPTEMBER 2015

She walks in beauty
—Lord Byron

The lovely
white silence of evening
as she walks darkly
through opening shadows
of night, hands
clasped behind her back
up a game trail of stars
wishing only
not to be seen
        tonight
as a goddess
but La Luna robed
gentle in the lifting palm
of twilight

for Jacoba and Dallas

LATE SEPTEMBER SONG

(upon seeing the first turning of the maple across the Cascade River)

All the redbirds gone
and the bowing trees blushweep
for the memory

for Jan, with love
20 September 2018
a new beginning

SUNRISE, BIRDS

an anniversary poem
August 13th

A small feather wind
sauntered its saucy way
into morning, then turned
with a soundless motion
and slipped into the hollow
behind its winged shadow

A young cloud
curved like a Canadian goose's neck
slowly swims the Comstock
over the sleeping woman skyline
ruffles the muttering crows
into bickerflutter

Suddenly a thousand fat bottlerocket quail
in contrapuntal symphony
burst through gathering light
thrusting flopping barrelrolling gliding
wake us flap flap chuckle flapping
into the fiftieth

(to be precise) year morning
gathering and gathering
singing the rhapsody of
soft tailwind and sky blue pink dawn
all the way to the nearest star
hanging golden on our lives' horizon

ACKNOWLEDGEMENTS
AND NOTES FROM THE BOAR'S NEST

Thanks to the following presses where poems in this collection
first appeared in book or chapbook form:

Copper Canyon Press
The Porcine Legacy (1978)
Driving and Drinking (1979)
The Porcine Canticles (1984)
Day's Work (1990)
My Town (1995)
A Legacy of Shadows (1999)
News From Down to the Café (1999)
So Quietly the Earth (2004)

Brooding Heron Press
Paragonah Canyon (1990)
Wayburne Pig (1997)

Spoon River Press
Covenants (with William Kloefkorn) (1996)

Wood Works Press
The Fish (1997)
Incident at Thompson Slough (2002)
Texas Wild Flowers (2011)

Logan House Press
In a House Made of Time (with William Kloefkorn) (2010)

Black Rock Press
Stone   Wind   Water (2011)

Wings Press
Moments of Delicate Balance
(with William Kloefkorn) (2011)

Last Call (2014)
Bluebonnets, Firewheels and Brown Eyed Susans (2017)

Five Sisters Press
Mine Tailings (2019)

Sugar House Press
The Allegory of Perfection (2020)

Normally, at this point in the Acknowledgements the poet presents a list of friends and associates who have been supportive or helpful in his/her development. I began that list and in fewer than thirty minutes inscribed the one hundredth name. Jan interrupted my desperation and told me to stop whining and just say right here, "I hope you know who you are and that you are dearly loved and appreciated." And Jan was once again spot on right.

Special thanks and acknowledgement to:

Rob Behunin, for assistance above and beyond the call of adopted brotherhood in the selection of poems and preparation of the manuscript for this book.

Sam Hamill and Tree Swenson, my first editors, amazing teachers and role models for perseverance, who launched me on this quest almost a half century ago.

My other beloved book-length editors who for reasons known to the gods were willing to take a chance on me over the years: Sam and Sally Green, David Pichaske, Paul Hunter, Chris Stern & Jules Remedios Faye, J. V. Brummels, Bob Blesse, Bryce Milligan, Nano Taggart, and Cheryl Cox.

My muses, William Kloefkorn and Eleanor Wilner, the profane and brilliant big brother and River Otter genius sister who reappeared from another life and reclaimed me as younger in-need sibling: abrazos y amor.
Steven Nightingale, the editor and publisher of this hopeful tome and potential door stop, for his amazing friendship and belief in me and for multiple life-regenerative residencies at the Place of

Owls and Granada Carmen.

Bob Blesse, who came out of retirement to design this book: I salute and from the heart thank you, sir.

Cheryl and the gang-October-family at the Cliff Notes writing conference, the finest small writing conference on the planet.

And I must acknowledge the literal thousands of students I have had the extreme pleasure to play and work in the fields of the Lord with over this long and ragged thing called a life. You have been my goal and reward and you, for better and/or worse, are responsible for who and what I have become. I tell you here: I gained far more than I gave. You are the reason. My career, my spirit, my life may well be summarized and perhaps justified by the following anonymous evaluation from one of my hundreds of classes taught at Southern Utah University:
"I enjoyed your class alot. I know this to be true that I know that I know more about poetry than anybody else in my family that do not read much poetry. I have to say though that I did not appreciate having to read the poem about the woman having sex with a duck. That was too far. But I liked and never missed your class. Never." And I know this to be true: there is a poet and a mythological figure out there in the ether named Yeats and Leda who love this comment as much as I do; of that fact I have not one scintilla of doubt. I love being in this company and I accept and adore this evaluation as Final Judgement.

May the gods bless you all.

About the Author

Born in west Texas, David Lee was Utah's first poet laureate; in 2001 he was a finalist for United States Poet Laureate. A former seminary student and semi-pro baseball player (the only white player to ever play in the Texas Negro Leagues for the Post, Texas Blue Stars) and hog farmer, he has a PhD. with a concentration in John Milton and taught at Southern Utah University for over three decades where he received every teaching award given by the university including being named Professor of the Year on three occasions.

His awards include multiple fellowships from the National Endowment for the Arts and the National Endowment for the Humanities, Western States Book Award, Mountain and Plains States Booksellers Award, Critics Choice Award, Utah Book Awards, Elkhorn Poetry Prize, Evolutionary Poem of the Year, Utah Governor's Award for Lifetime Achievement in the Arts, Utah Governor's Merit Award in the Humanities and an Honorary Doctorate of Humane Letters. The Utah Humanities Council and Utah Education Association named him one of the top twelve writers in Utah literary history and he was the fifth academic in Utah higher education to be named a Lifetime Fellow by the Utah Academy of Arts and Sciences.

About the Artist

Cover artist Phyllis Shafer is a plein air landscape painter who taught at Lake Tahoe Community College since 1994. She received her Master of Fine Arts degree from the University of California, Berkeley, and has exhibited her work nationally and internationally since 1984. Her work is based on a belief that a kind of transcendental essence lies at the heart of all natural forms and objects—through the process of painting, her artistic goal is to distill and crystallize that essence and the vital rhythms that animate it.

Colophon

The text typeface is Arno, created by Robert Slimbach at Adobe. The typeface is named for the Arno River, which flows through the center of Florence, Italy. It is an old-style font, inspired by 15th and 16th typefaces and described by the designer as a combination of Aldine and Venetian styles; its italic was inspired by the work of Ludovico degli Arrighi, a Renaissance type designer. In 2006, Arno received an award in typeface design from the Type Designers Club of New York.

The display typeface on the cover and titling is Mrs. Eaves, a transitional serif typeface designed by Zuzana Licko in 1996. It is a revival of the types of English printer and punchcutter John Baskerville, and is named for his longtime housekeeper and collaborator, Sarah Eaves, whom eventually became his wife.

The calligraphic typeface on the cover is Rialto, designed by Austrian Lui Karner and Venetian Giovanni de Faccio in 1995. It is named for the famous bridge in Venice, Italy.

Designed and produced by Robert Blesse

Printed and bound by McNaughton & Gunn, Saline, MI

This is the first publication of Samara Press